W9-BQX-077

Effective Urban Church Ministry

EFFECTIVE URBAN CHURCH MINISTRY

G. Willis Bennett

BROADMAN PRESS
Nashville, Tennessee

© Copyright 1983 • Broadman Press
All rights reserved

4255-26
ISBN: 0-8054-5526-4

Dewey Decimal Classification: 253.22
Subject heading: CITY CHURCHES

Library of Congress Catalog Card Number: 83-70370
Printed in the United States of America

CENTER
FOR
URBAN
CHURCH
STUDIES

The Center for Urban Church Studies was begun in 1981 as a cooperative effort of the Sunday School Board, Foreign Mission Board, Home Mission Board, Brotherhood Commission, Woman's Missionary Union, and the six seminaries of the Southern Baptist Convention. The Center was created to conduct research and compile information on the urban areas of the world in order to gain greater understanding and knowledge of how the gospel can most effectively be shared in these large urban areas.

70631

Foreword

We all have an idea of what a truly effective urban church should look like, but often there persists the nagging feeling that such an ideal congregation just cannot exist in the city, much less in the inner city. Is it possible for a church in the inner city to reach its community, to grow in numbers and in stature, to be a moral force for social change, and to provide a compassionate ministry for those in need? Mission agencies and seminary professors have been encouraging churches toward this ideal for years, but often doubting that the churches they advise or the pastors they train will ever aspire to the goal of developing an effective urban church.

Give us a model! This is a call we often hear, because people will believe something is possible only if they can see it in action. So, in this book a model is presented of an effective urban church.

This is not the first time Allen Temple Baptist Church in Oakland, California, has been offered as a model. I have been a close observer of the church for ten years and on numerous occasions have taken pastors, directors of associational missions, state convention leaders, and others to this church in order to show them the breadth of its ministry and the vitality of its pastor and congregation. Others have done the same, and the reputation of Allen Temple has spread far beyond the Bay area of California. But too few church leaders will ever have the opportunity to visit this church, and so the idea was born to have someone capture the mission, ministry, and outreach of Allen Temple Baptist Church in book form.

The Center for Urban Church Studies was fortunate that Dr. G. Willis Bennett from The Southern Baptist Theological Seminary was willing to give part of his sabbatical to do an in-depth study of Allen Temple. Dr. Bennett draws from his eighteen years of pastoral experience, more than twenty-five years of experience as a consultant to churches throughout the United States, and twenty-four years of teaching experience at Southern Seminary to accomplish this task. Before he visited Allen Temple, Dr. Bennett did not feel a significant book on a single church was warranted, or perhaps even possible. His view changed, however, after the first contact with this amazing church. Yet in a very real sense this book is not simply a model of an effective urban church, it is an effort to demonstrate principles of effective urban ministry. The book is a blend of theory and action, principles and examples. A theoretical approach makes it applicable to any urban setting, and the example of Allen Temple brings it to life and shows that the truly effective urban church is a reality.

I am sure that there are many other effective urban churches in our world, but I know of no other that more completely exemplifies what the church ought to be than Allen Temple—from their dynamic worship experience, to serious Bible study, to personal evangelism, to community ministry. Many churches have made headlines in church growth materials only to falter in a few years. The Allen Temple story is one that has stood the test of time. Ministry in the urban setting is not easy and there are no quick and simple solutions to the problems it presents. A church must be committed to the long haul, not sacrificing one aspect of mission for another.

While Allen Temple is not the perfect church, it does provide a dynamic model of how a church can minister in the urban setting. The principles outlined by Dr. Bennett and the examples of Allen Temple can be utilized by any church desiring to be effective, regardless of size or location.

Allen Temple is historically a black church. However, the reader should not simplistically say that such a fact "explains" what they are doing or why they have been successful in their community. To do so is to misunderstand the primary reasons for their effectiveness. There are many other churches in Oakland: Black, Hispanic, Anglo, and other ethnic groups, but we know of none which has had the effective ministry of Allen Temple.

It is my feeling that all churches can profit by the principles outlined in the book and the Allen Temple model, and I hope you will find this book both stimulating and inspiring. I also hope you will be challenged to make your church a model of effective urban ministry. It will not be easy nor will success come quickly. It is my desire that this book will be a tool for your church as it seeks to minister to our urban world.

I express my personal appreciation to Dr. J. Alfred Smith and the Allen Temple family for allowing us to conduct this research project. Their openness and genuine Christian spirit have given me encouragement; in spite of all the obstacles in the city, a church willing to pay the price of commitment can be effective in sharing the good news of the gospel.

I also thank Dr. G. Willis Bennett who has given his time, energy, and expertise to this project. It was a privilege to work with him, as always.

LARRY ROSE
Executive Director,
Center for Urban Church Studies
Spring, 1983

Preface

Many of my friends and former students function as Christian ministers in cities scattered all across the United States. They have shared with me their joys and successes, as well as their trials and frustrations. Some of them have participated in urban church conferences with me and frequently have challenged me to place in writing some of the ideas which I have shared. This book is an effort to accomplish that goal, in hopes that some of the ideas might prove useful to those committed ministers and lay Christians who serve in urban places. I am deeply convinced that the Christian church serves as a source of hope for our cities. I believe in the value of congregational ministries and would like strongly to affirm faithful pastors and others who continue to provide creative leadership. This book I humbly offer as one contribution toward the enhancement of redemptive efforts in the cities.

My deepest appreciation is warmly given to those who have made this book possible. First, I thank The Southern Baptist Theological Seminary for the opportunity of developing and refining many of these ideas during the years that I have taught church and community, and for providing a sabbatical that has made the research and writing possible. The Center for Urban Church Studies, of the Southern Baptist Convention, is responsible for suggesting to me that I write a book which would allow the use of a case study of an effective church. Larry Rose, executive director of the Center, and his staff provided valuable counsel and assistance. Furthermore, the Center provided financial support to make the case study possible.

Particular gratitude is expressed to the Allen Temple Baptist Church of Oakland, California, and to the pastor, Dr. J. Alfred Smith. These kind people gave maximum cooperation and support to my research and writing. My appreciation to them will never end, and they shall continue to be a source of inspiration.

My wife, Caroline, faithful companion throughout my adult life, has been a constant source of encouragement. Her love and understanding have provided acceptance and support so necessary for the completion of this project.

Appreciation is expressed also to three persons who have provided essential assistance. Nenette Measels and Sharon White, competent secretaries and understanding friends, have given generously to those daily tasks that are required in our continuing work. Terri Lynn Mathews has been the typist of the manuscript at each stage of its development, and I express my thanks to her both for her skill and pleasant manner.

G. WILLIS BENNETT
Louisville, Kentucky

Contents

1/Introducing an Approach to Church Ministry

On a rainy January night 135 persons were gathered in the fellowship hall of the Allen Temple Baptist Church. Open Bibles and notebooks were on tables before them. Pastor J. Alfred Smith was at the lecturn near the blackboard where he was intently engaged in teaching the Book of Romans. This was a weekly occasion where people gathered for two hours of serious Bible study. They followed an outline which had been distributed. They engaged in recitations in response to questions, and they raised questions of their own. Implications for life in our day were suggested and explained. This was Bible teaching for lay Christians at its best.

The Bible lesson for the evening concluded, the group shared briefly some common concerns. One had experienced a death in the family. Another had lost his job, and the group joined in encouragement and support with the promise to try to help him find work and to make certain that his needs were supplied until work was found. The group prayed for each other and for the wider concerns of the community and the world.

Then before bringing the service to a close everyone stood, and the pastor invited any person present who wanted to receive the Lord Jesus as Savior to come forward, or if one wanted to become a member of the church he or she should come. Four adults immediately came forward. There was no music, no pressure, just the

15

warmth of the fellowship, the presence of the Spirit, and a receptive congregation prepared to extend fellowship to any sincere believer.

After the reception of the new members, the congregation joined hands, had a prayer, broke into song, and then adjourned. No one seemed in any hurry to leave, and the joyful sharing in which they engaged gave evidence of their sense of belonging to each other.

The experience affirmed what I had already come to believe. Here was a church where God is at work, where people love one another, and where there is a commitment to reach out and bear witness to the gospel. Surely there is a story here worth telling, a model for ministry worth sharing. I resolved to try to tell that story, and this book is the outcome.

The title to this book suggests a pragmatic approach. How can one make urban church ministry effective? Ministers and laypersons alike want a ministry that "works." They have grown tired of seeing churches decline in the city and dissipate their energies with apparently little to show for their efforts. Pastoral search committees sometimes ask questions which seem to call for an idea or a plan that would suggest the prospective minister knows at the outset the magic formula for quick success. Frequently pastors, themselves weary from their own unfruitful labors, turn to finding an associate or other new staff minister who will be able both to bring relief and inject new enthusiasm into the church. And so it goes in many urban places.

Our pragmatism makes us search for an approach, process, or model which will show us the way to ultimate success in our church work. Of course, much may hinge upon what we call "success" or upon the question regarding when urban ministry can be said to be "effective." Is our judgment to be based upon a quantitative measurement? When the church is able to reach more people than during the previous year, shall we call it successful and effective? When there is evidence that evangelism has reaped the rewards of increased baptisms and therefore new church membership growth, shall we say we have become an effective church? When financial records show increased giving, and the church is able to meet financial obligations and even increase missionary support, shall we declare that we have had a successful year? Surely these quantitative measurements are important, and they do say something about long-term survival. Local congregations and denominations will continue to measure the vitality of a church, at least in part, by examining the numerical records.

There also are other measurements that ought to be used. A congregation needs to be certain that it has agreed upon a valid theology for its ministry. Thereafter, everything it does in witness and ministry should be in accord with that theology. As the people of God on mission with Christ in the world, the church has a task unlike that of any other organization or institution. A congregation needs to claim its true identity and determine its God-given purpose, and then it needs continually to design its witness and ministry in a way that will enable it to be faithful to what it perceives it is called to be and to do. Repeated review and evaluation should enable a judgment to be made as to the church's faithfulness to these commitments. In the light of those findings, admittedly very difficult to ascertain, the church can get some idea as to its effectiveness. This judgment may or may not coincide with the numerical determinants of success.

Methods of Study

This book, therefore, will deal with some pragmatic questions, but these will be approached from the standpoint of biblical theology and a philosophy and theory of urban church work that it is hoped will provide a basis for "effective" church ministry. The best sources of urban church research to be found in literary documents have been examined through years of teaching in the field of church and community. Personal visitation through the years with churches located in the major urban areas of our nation provides a source of experience that will be tapped. However, I have not been content to rely upon present knowledge and past experience. Rather, I have chosen to weave throughout the theology and theory of this book the insights gained from a current case study of a church which generally is recognized as being effective. This case material will be used in each chapter to illustrate the theory of ministry that has been advanced. One church, rather than many, has been used so as to give an in-depth analysis of how theology and theory can be applicable in a given setting. When success has been experienced, it will be documented, and limitations and needs which still exist will be noted.

The church used in the case study is the Allen Temple Baptist Church of Oakland, California. Allen Temple was begun as the 85th Avenue Baptist Church in 1919, a church affiliated with the Northern Baptist Convention. The first pastor of the twenty-one-member congregation was J. L. Allen, who served the church until 1925. Not long after his departure the congregation changed the name of the church to Allen Temple Baptist Church. Through the years the church has been served by a total of seven pastors, the current one being Dr. J. Alfred Smith who came to the pastorate in 1970. The church is now affiliated with the Progressive National Baptist Convention, as well as the American Baptist Convention, USA. It has grown to a membership of more than 2800, representing more than 1100 families. Other appropriate information drawn from the case study of this church will be found in each of the chapters which follow.

The approach to the case study explains also the general structure of this book. When making a case study, or in serving as a consultant to a church, I try in various ways to determine the answer to four general questions. These are:

1. Who are we as a congregation? Who are we in terms of our theology and our human makeup?

2. Where are we as a congregation? Where are we in terms of historic time and geographic place?

3. What are we doing as a congregation, and how well are we doing it?

4. What ought we to be doing as a congregation, and how are we to do it?

The first question causes one to explore the theological nature of a congregation in terms of its recognized statements of belief and in terms of its actual practice as observed or otherwise detected. It also leads one to look at the church as a social group. Whatever a church may be theologically as it claims to be a "congregation of the Lord," it is also a collection of human beings with names, faces, interests, needs, and aspirations. These persons have joined themselves together, gain support from one another, and collectively carry on the work of God in a given place.

The second question provides the opportunity to examine the uniqueness of a church in light of its history and its social setting. How has a church emerged in time, and what are the strands of history that provide continuity? In terms of place, what are the characteristics determined by the social setting? Every church is located within a community, and the nature of that community inevitably provides the opportunities for the church and the limitations upon it.

An examination of the programs and activities of a congregation provides the answer to question 3. These activities are to be identified, observed, and described. They serve as a validation of what a congregation claims to be in its own statements of faith and self-description. Some type of evaluation needs to be made of the activities, so as to affirm their ability to accomplish their stated purpose, or to determine wherein they fail. Evaluation of any program is difficult and perhaps always somewhat subjective. Certainly, however, it is of value to document how activities and programs are perceived by observers and by those who are participants.

The final question leads one to examine a congregation's ability to plan for continuity, change, and new directions. What new dreams come into focus? Is there imagination among the people, and particularly among the leadership? If it is impossible to secure some direction for the future, can this then begin to take the design of a blueprint? Strategies that suggest methodologies for witness and ministry, if indeed they exist, are to be identified. If they do not exist, assistance may be needed to see if they can be developed. The future of any congregation is conditioned by its ability to dream and translate the dream into reality.

In trying to use these questions as a research approach to the Allen Temple Church, the author spent an extended period of time with the church and community. Documents pertaining to the church's history and its current organization and ministry were examined with care. Individual and group interviews were conducted with key leaders and with representative members. Some interviews deliberately were with persons whose membership spanned more than twenty years and some with those of less than two years. The interviews represented male and female, persons of all ages, and persons of various educational and economic levels. Some were picked at random, while others were included because of their leadership roles. Some interviews were formally structured; others were more casual and informal, such as during visits into the homes of members for meals and conversation.

A questionnaire was also used with the congregation to solicit both information and attitudinal response toward the church and its ministry. These unsigned responses were intended to provide a more scientific measurement to supplement the data gathered through interviews and observation.

Being a participant-observer in worship services, prayer meeting, Bible study, business meetings, and training and group activities made it possible to form some impressions about the vitality of the church and its ministry. Further insights were gained simply by observing the pastor and the office staff at work, and in seeing the lay members come and go daily in their participation in weekday activities and volunteer work.

The case study was not limited to the internal life of the congregation. The immediate community and the city as a whole were studied. This was done through examination of the 1980 census material appropriate for an understanding of the church's social setting. Visitation to schools, apartment buildings, businesses, and recreational centers in the immediate community served by the church proved helpful. By appointments, interviews were conducted with several persons in the city who were not members of the congregation but were in positions to assess the contribution of the church to the community. These included other ministers, educators, city councilmen, the mayor, the publisher of the major newspaper, public officials, and some professional persons who work in the delivery of human services.

The study of this congregation and its community has been done in more depth and detail than normally would be given during a typical consultant's work with a church. This has been done in order to secure reliable information, but also to allow the author to gain a "feel" for this congregation in order to see it from the inside as well as from without. In the pages that follow I will not burden the reader with unnecessary documentation but shall try to present a truthful and thorough picture of one church. Drawing from this material, we shall be able to see the application of the principles and theories advanced within these chapters.

Foundational Theory for the Study

The contention that it is possible to plan and realize effective urban church ministry is founded upon certain assumptions which need to be identified. Those who plan and direct the ministry of a church need to possess a happy combination of several highly significant ingredients. Figure 1 is intended to identify the ingredients and to imply their interrelatedness.[1]

It is almost impossible to plan for effective church ministry unless one has an awareness of the social setting in which that ministry is to be performed. Who are the people providing the ministry, and to whom are they providing it? Who are the people whom a particular congregation is attempting to reach, and what are they like? Will it help to know their ages, sex, educational level, interests, needs, and other social data that may help one know how to anticipate their receptivity to a given ministry? This kind of data is what is meant by "sociological awareness."

Already emphasis has been given to theological understanding. We who plan ministry do need to understand the nature and mission of the church. We need also to understand what God would have us do in today's world and whether or not there is a word from God to the

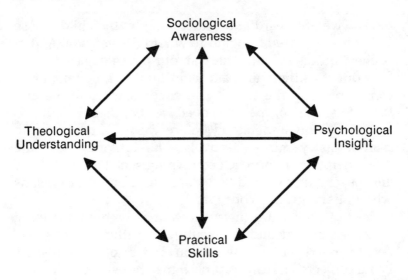

Figure 1: Leadership Ingredients

persons living in the city. "Oh, yes!" we say. But sometimes we have difficulty knowing how to convey God's
care and concern to some of the troubled persons we meet.
We may resort to giving the psychological answer, or to
making the political effort, and forget that Christian ministry will not do less but will search also for the theological
meaning and the godly word and deed. This must always
be one of the ingredients of leadership, not in isolation
from the other but interacting with them.

Ministers need an adequate knowledge of psychology.
See, for example, how important it is to relate psychological insight to the other factors under consideration. We
need to try to understand the reactions of persons to our
words and actions. For example, it is theologically valid to
speak of God as Father and to use the term to talk of his
care and protection. We need to be sensitive, however, as

to how we are heard and understood by the child whose father has deserted him and to whom the very thought of "father" brings resentment. Can our psychological insight feed our sensitivity and aid us in finding a better way of communicating the truth? The circumstances of life and the life-styles of people need to be discovered, interpreted, and understood before we will know how to plan ministry more effectively. The importance of the interdisciplinary approach combining sociology, theology, and psychology should be evident to thoughtful persons who understand the concepts.

Practical skills are always essential both in planning effective ministry and in executing it. Sufficient skills may be possessed within one person, but in other ministries being projected a team approach may be essential in order to capture all the skills required. The most obvious illustration points toward using persons with certain types of gifts to engage in research. Others with a different type of gift may be used in interpretation of the data and planning of ministry. Still others may become the ones to engage in the ministry on a daily basis. If not all are theologically and psychologically sensitive, maybe another can try to inject these insights into the ministry component. Perhaps the term *practical skills* is not adequate to describe fully the intended meaning. I mean the possession of whatever gift is required to enable the theory to be put into practice—the ministry to be implemented.

Overview of Content of Chapters

The four questions addressed earlier in this chapter are interlocked with the four concepts projected above. Throughout the remaining chapters, these ideas will reoccur as appropriate. A brief overview of the chapters may point the direction to be followed.

In chapter 2 the scriptural bases for the nature and

purpose of the church are presented as the foundation upon which effective church ministry is based. Illustrations from Allen Temple Church will examine its theological statements and the relationship of the commitments to its ministry.

The importance of congregational identity, the discovery of ministry possibilities, and the way a church engages in ministry become the subjects treated in chapters 3, 4, and 5. These chapters reveal how one church conducted research to enable it to find the answers related to priorities for ministry and then engage in a ministry that has proved highly effective.

Chapter 6 enables us to look at factors contributing to the remarkable growth of Allen Temple. In the context of the chapter, the concept of intentionality as related to evangelism and church growth is explained.

The training and use of committed Christians in ministry is the focus of chapter 7. Strength for a church resides in its ability to lead its people to discover and use their spiritual gifts. The special programs of annual lay training at Allen Temple are described.

Chapter 8 stresses the importance of worship in the life of a church. It contains a discussion of the importance of designing worship in a manner that will enable it to be faithful to a valid theology without losing its cultural relevance. The dynamic services at Allen Temple are described and analyzed.

No book on church ministry is complete apart from the recognition of the importance of the role of the pastor. This topic is explored in chapter 9, with particular attention to the work of J. Alfred Smith, pastor of Allen Temple.

The concluding chapter explores the importance of a congregation examining its existing situation and projecting its ministry for the future. Perhaps the number one neglect in most churches is the failure of the church to engage in periodic and effective evaluation of its programs and ministry. Some suggestions and forms of evaluation are provided and those used at Allen Temple are examined. Under the title "Dreaming New Dreams," future planning for the church and the motivation and method of engaging in planning are described. Illustrations from within the Allen Temple congregation are used.

It will be seen, therefore, that ministry theory and ministry practice are blended within every chapter of this book. The intention has been to set forth a method of engaging in urban church ministry and to illustrate that method with a church model, one we believe must be viewed as having proved to be effective.[2]

NOTES

1. These concepts also may be found in literature setting forth the approach of the Association for Christian Training and Service (ACTS), Nashville, Tennessee, and the Urban Training Cooperative, Home Mission Board of the Southern Baptist Convention, Atlanta, Georgia. Both organizations' founding committees were chaired by the writer. Both serve in the field of church consultations, working with individual congregations and with groups of churches. ACTS is regional and ecumenical, while UTC confines its work largely to the Southern Baptist Convention.

2. The reader will understand that using Allen Temple Baptist Church as a model is not a recommendation that all urban churches try to duplicate programs and activities discussed in this volume. Try to learn from what is here and apply what you learn to the areas in which you minister.

2/Building Upon Theological Foundations

One dominant factor which makes the church different from other social groups is its identification with Jesus Christ. It claims to have been founded by him, and it proposes to join Christ in the world in ministry in his name. It draws its mandate from the teaching of Jesus and its energy from the Holy Spirit. The church is unique. Drawing from the Bible, it indeed makes an effort to build upon theological foundations.

Now the statements above are the ideal, and the degree to which a local congregation is successful in acting seriously upon them may very well determine the effectiveness of that congregation. Let us look then at how a congregation may claim this identity for itself and return again and again to reaffirm its faith.

Most congregations at the time they are constituted as a church accept some statement or articles of faith. It may become a part of a constitution, or a covenant. Perhaps also the congregation has other statements of purpose which have been designed and approved from time to time. Any such statements should not be taken lightly but should become the foundation upon which a church structures its objectives and plans its ministry.

While it will not be possible in this present consideration to treat the theological concerns in much length or depth, it is appropriate to provide a summary statement to indicate several highly important concepts which a congregation ought to include in its understanding.

The Nature of the Church

Any theological foundation upon which a church should build needs to contain an acceptable interpretation of the church from a biblical point of view. The roots of the Christian church may be traced to the Old Testament. God's covenant relationship with Israel designated the people as special, as is seen in the Hebrew phrase *Yahweh gahal*, usually translated "assembly of the Lord" or "congregation of the Lord." Having been "elected" or "called" into a special relationship, the people were expected to be "separate from" the world or "separate to" Jehovah.[1] In the Septuagint, *gahal* usually is translated *ekklesia* which later becomes the word used in the New Testament in reference to the church. The idea of the covenant became a focal point for the beliefs of Israel, and it is not surprising to find the early Christians interpreting themselves as people of the new covenant (Heb. 10:16).

At least two words from the New Testament must be understood to capture the essence of the church: *ekklesia* and *koinonia*.[2] In the Septuagint, *ekklesia* referred to the people who had come together for religious purposes, such as for worship. In the New Testament the word was used to designate Christians who were gathered as the people of God to do the work for which they believed Jesus had established his church. Like Israel before them, they were to be a "household of faith" (Gal. 6:10), "the temple of the living God" (2 Cor. 6:16), "the body of Christ" (1 Cor. 12:27; Rom. 12; Eph. 4:4-16). They like Israel felt themselves called, and they were to be separated to God and from the world.

The other word *koinonia* generally is translated as "fellowship," and has the meaning of sharing. For New Testament Christians, this was a sharing in friendship, faith, the work of Christ, and even in the sharing of possessions (Acts 2:44). It was a fellowship instigated and governed by the Holy Spirit. It was a bond that joined Christians to each other, to Christ, and to God.[3] Paul's strong emphasis upon community probably results from his deep commitment to the concept of *koinonia*.

Any congregation needs the two concepts to be the core of its perception of itself. Having become members of Christ through their response to his call, they also become members of one another through the power of the Holy Spirit. This church is built by Christ, not by humans. Persons may be added to it and may come to represent and to manifest it, but it is Christ who calls it into existence.[4] Indeed, this truth is the basis for our confidence in the permanence of the church. Christ is the author, and the church is here to stay. The form and structure that the church takes may change, for indeed the church is still in the process of becoming. It is not a finished product, not a static institution. The church is a living organism and is still "being built," but its life has the guarantee of Christ himself. Local congregations may disband and disappear, but the church of Jesus Christ shall last forever.

The Purpose of the Church

While form and structure of the church may change, it seems logical to claim that the purpose of the church does not change. The way in which the church's purpose is implemented may change in the light of new circumstances and particular situations. Even the various functions that the church may undertake to fulfill may change and expand, but the purpose for which those functions exist remains essentially the same.

However one may choose to describe the purpose of the church, Paul's phrase in Ephesians should not be neglected. "We who first hoped in Christ have been destined and appointed to live for the praise of his glory" (Eph.

1:12). To glorify God forever is a continuing and unending purpose of the church, and all that the church is and everything it does should serve this purpose. Paul's writings make it clear that he thought this purpose incorporated both an inward stance toward others who were of the household of faith and an outward thrust of witness and ministry to the world. Thus, most statements of faith include the concept of how the "body of believers" have been joined together by Christ into a covenant of faith and fellowship, and are to be committed to the witness and service of Christ so as to extend the gospel to the ends of the earth.

The purpose of the church, therefore, is related to fellowship (*koinonia*) and to service (*diakonia*). The church's witness in the world depends upon both *being* and *doing*. The very fact that the church exists within itself is a witness to the glory of God. To be the people of God, to demonstrate the presence of the Spirit, to exist in unity wherein love prevails, to share freely in a community of faith—these bring glory to God and bear witness to his name. A pagan world could marvel, "See how they love one another!" Such evidence in our day also bears witness to the truth of God's power.

Being will lead ultimately to *doing*. By deliberate design, a church committed to a valid theological purpose will wish to engage in functions that fit the category of service (*diakonia*). Many treatises on this topic speak of the *mission* of the church. Dale Moody has expressed it pointedly: "The church is mission, and where there is no mission there is no church. God has called the church out from the world to send her back into the world with a message and a mission."[5]

The church must be careful not to confuse ends and means. It seems that sometimes a congregation may make its own institutional existence the end rather than the means. The end must be the glorifying of God, the reconciliation of all persons to the Father through the Lord Jesus Christ, and the doing of the Father's will. The congregation as a social group, therefore, must never become the end, but the means whereby the end is accomplished. This concept deserves further explanation as the mission of the church is examined in the context of looking at some of its functions.

The Functions of the Church

For churches in the first century, and for many churches throughout history, certain definite functions have been fulfilled in very practical ways. Some of these seem absolutely essential if the church is to be faithful to its mission. Several are identified below.

The one function of the church which probably is most common to all congregations is that of providing opportunities for the worship of God on the part of the gathered congregation. If God is to be glorified, provision must be made for the faithful to come before him with praises and in obedience. Ministers, acting upon the traditions of biblical priests and prophets, arrange for services of worship in which the Word of God is proclaimed and the petitions of the people are offered to God. The Bible, the written source of religious authority, becomes the textual material for instruction. The people are encouraged to reverence God in their celebration, to call upon his name, and to commit themselves to his will. Worship at its best unites the believer with God and relates all believers who share in the celebration.

The church also is to call persons to experience newness of life in Christ. Evangelism, therefore, becomes a crucial function. While it may be related to a worship service, it is not to be confined in that manner. Evangelism involves "doing" as well as "saying," because witness is not solely at the mercy of the proclamation of words either by a preacher or by some other individual. The church must witness in deeds as well as words. Making disciples, baptizing them, and teaching them form a part of the evangelistic task. It is important for a congregation to be committed to the fulfillment of this task, and to approach it with intentionality.

A church is expected to instruct its members in the ways of Christ and in the knowledge of Christian living. This religious educational function of the church is vital both to the growth of spirituality within the congregation and for impact upon nonmembers who have been encouraged to participate.

The fellowship function serves to enable a congregation to provide through association with fellow Christians the kind of encouragement and support which are essential for personal growth. It is in the setting of the fellowship that members also can best be confronted and disciplined in the faith. The art of reconciliation deserves development if a congregation is to fulfill the intention of true *koinonia*. The teaching of Paul regarding the Lord's Supper emphasizes both the relationship to Christ and to each other, and the observance of the Supper is an opportunity to strengthen the fellowship. Within the fellowship function, and sometimes related to the Lord's Supper in many churches, is the provision of economic assistance to members in need and to those beyond the fellowship.

The admonition to the church to extend its witness to the ends of the earth suggests the importance of the missionary function. While this function is also to be identified with evangelism, it may be treated separately because of the command to reach beyond the boundaries of the immediate community. The extension of the witness comes primarily through the sending of others, as the early church sent Paul and his associates. Prayerful, financial, and other personal support provide the means for the fulfillment of this function.

One other function deserving serious consideration is the church's efforts to fashion a personal and social environment wherein its members and other human beings shall be able to realize the potential which God intends for his children. Sometimes the social structures which humans encounter tend to dehumanize, degrade, and otherwise hamper the realization of the abundant life Christ wants people to experience. The faithful church will cry out for social justice and will attempt to become an instrument for change that will help redeem the structures of society and join Christ in ministry within the world. In recent years some churches have identified this function as the Christian social ministry or social action component of their ministry. They have related it to the effort to act upon their Christian ethical concerns, to witness in deed and not in word only.

These functions—worship, evangelism, education, fellowship, missionary, and Christian social ministry and action—are the functions which seem minimal for the church which wants to be found faithful. While other functions could be specified, it is possible for these six to form broad categories that could well include the others in a fuller discussion. In succeeding chapters we shall return to some of these ideas, especially as we explore how one church approached its mission.

Foundational Theology
for Allen Temple Baptist Church

The Allen Temple Baptist Church has a constitution which alludes to theology at several points but specifically anchors its faith on two statements found in the Preamble and in Article II. The Preamble reads in part:

> Reposing our faith wholly in the Lord Jesus Christ of
> our salvation, believing in the teachings and practices
> of the Baptists and in those great distinctive principals
> for which they have ever stood. . . .[6]

The document then records ten principals, not all inci-
dentally "distinctive" to Baptists, but stressing basic fun-
damentals to which the church is prepared to commit
itself: the preeminence of Christ as Lord and Master, the
supreme authority of the Bible, the competency of the
individual to approach God directly, the separation of
church and state, a regenerate church membership, believer's baptism, congregational autonomy, majority rule
in church government, spiritual unity of believers, and a
commitment to missions and evangelism.

These, it can be seen, set a rather definite direction and
are specific enough to identify the congregation as a
Christian body intent upon knowing who it is and what it
is about.

The statement of purpose is contained in Article II:

> The purpose of this church shall be the advancement of the
> Kingdom of Jesus Christ. It shall seek to attain this goal
> through the public worship of God, the preaching of the
> Gospel, consistent Christian living by its members, per-
> sonal evangelism, missionary endeavor, and Christian edu-
> cation.

The focus of this church's purpose is related to Christ, the
founder, and six objectives are used to indicate the direction of effort in moving toward the ultimate goal of "the
advancement of the Kingdom of Christ."

The point I wish to make here is not the wording of a
statement of purpose but the importance of one. Ob-
viously, we want to see a statement which will be viewed
as theologically valid. Not all churches would agree to the

same wording, or even the intent. It is not necessary to have uniformity. Theology will vary between denominations, and even among churches within a denomination. However, the point I am making is upon the importance of a congregation knowing who it is theologically and being in agreement upon its basic objectives. That will provide a point of reference to which the congregation may return from time to time to reassure itself of its direction. Evaluation of the church's witness and ministry may then be made in light of the purpose that has been predetermined.

No formal statement, particularly a relatively brief one, can be adequate to provide the theological foundation being discussed in this chapter. Within a congregation there will be elaborations upon their beliefs; and those may be found in other documents, especially in the kind of instruction used to indoctrinate the people. Perhaps the sermons preached by the pastor, or material prepared by him, will indicate what the people are called upon to be and to believe.

At Allen Temple Church such a document is found in a printed booklet, "The Local Church in God's Mission." It contains a paper by the pastor and a report by the president of the church's Women's Mission Society. A preface says that Pastor Smith's paper "provides a theoretical basis for such ministries as revealed in the Biblical roots and the historical, philosophical, theological legacy of classic Christian thought." It is set forth to reveal "the style of Allen Temple's ministry" in the light of their own theological commitments.

Pastor Smith pleads for a church which will be "the visible manifestation of the invisible Christ" and will accept a "servant-church theology." He would like to see a church with an "harmonious balance between faith and works, theology and practice" and one that is "committed to cultivating rich inner spirituality as well as courageous action outside of themselves for social justice."

In another paper entitled "Turning a Community Upside Down Through Worship and Ministry," the pastor shows how the church seeks to integrate its objectives. He describes the need to hold many types of diverse people together through worship and to use that worship to address the varied needs that those people have. He declares:

> You see, at Allen Temple, the church assembled is concerned about regeneration and racism, hell and housing, justification and justice, evangelism and ecology, prayer and poverty.

But in every worship service, the pastor claims, "the gospel will be preached, the afflicted will be comforted, and the invitation to accept Jesus Christ as Lord and Savior will be given."

In "Program Report, 1977," a booklet dealing with a description of programs, needs, and priorities at a time the congregation was considering a building program, several sections treated church concerns related to worship, education, fellowship, recreation, administration, outreach, and facilities. A strong emphasis was placed upon "theological rationale" or "theological concepts." Each group engaged in the study apparently had been expected to relate a given program to a valid theology. For example, the statement related to Christian education reads:

> As baptized believers, we propose that the message of the preeminence of Christ, as our Divine Lord and Master, the supreme authority of the Bible, and its sufficiency as our only rule of faith and practice, be communicated through formal and informal educational programs, so that individuals respond by personal faith in Christ and grow toward spiritual maturity.

These illustrations show how the pastor and people at Allen Temple tried to be faithful to their statement of purpose and objectives. There are continual serious efforts to root their programs and actions upon the biblical and theological concepts they have accepted for themselves.

In writing about "The Bold Mission of the Church," the pastor contended that Bold Mission proceeds upon five basic assumptions:

1. The local church is an important Christian community for accomplishing God's mission in the world.
2. Members of the local church need to be trained by the pastor to work harmoniously in order to accomplish God's mission in the world.
3. God's mission concerns itself with the personal acceptance of Jesus as Lord and Savior, and this mission shares God's deepest concern for justice, human worth, and dignity.
4. Commitment to God's mission requires a holy boldness on public issues of morality and ethics, and this boldness, when necessary, takes a strong stand against spiritual wickedness in the high places of power in the nation and world.
5. Bold mission in the local church means the membership is prepared to accept the life-style and philosophy of Jesus Christ, while rejecting the life-style, false gods, and living standards of popular culture.[7]

The pastor added, "Bold mission . . . acknowledges the preeminence of the Holy Spirit in church development. . . . Without God's power no church will be the *church on mission.*"[8]

These writings and the previous statements are only a few that indicate a conscious effort on the part of a congregation and its leadership to express its beliefs and commitments. They may not satisfy others but they serve the purpose at Allen Temple to provide a basis for action.

One may note that of the six functions set forth as minimal for the faithful church, Allen Temple addresses each of them in one way or another. The fellowship function is stressed in the Preamble to the constitution; worship, evangelism, education, and missions are all addressed in Article II. The emphasis upon Christian social ministry and action, while not by that name, is a major part of the work of deacons and a committee. Other statements recorded above strongly stress social justice and the need for a caring congregation.

It is evident that these people have thought about who they are as a religious body, and what they are to do. Perhaps at some future date they will want to review their statements and expand them. For now, they seek to act upon them, as will be documented in succeeding chapters.

Distinctions for Consideration

Any congregation which is a part of an ecclesiastical body with a common statement of beliefs and practices may be required to follow that statement as its own. In such case, the congregation should make sure of its own understanding and commitment. For congregations within denominational structures allowing local church autonomy, such as is true of Allen Temple and other Baptist churches, these congregations should establish their own theological frame of reference. While it will need to be in harmony with the general beliefs adhered to by the denomination with which the church is affiliated, there may be unique features. Baptist churches traditionally have allowed for considerable diversity. It becomes all the more important, therefore, for a particular congregation to make sure of its own identity.

A congregation may choose to adopt for itself some statement of faith used by other congregations, statements found in the New Hampshire Confession (1833), or the Statement of the Baptist Faith and Message adopted by the Southern Baptist Convention in 1963. Even if this is done, it is important to understand the statement and to instruct the congregation in it. Beyond such statements, the need still exists for a congregation to mark out with clearness what it perceives to be its purpose and objectives.

There is a limit as to how complete and adequate such formal statements may be. As seen in the Allen Temple example, some additional statements, if representative of the church, provide a richer understanding of what the congregation commits itself to do.

From time to time, a congregation needs to define how its formal statements of faith relate to specific programs and efforts. Its projection of activities, expenditure of effort, and disbursement of funds should be consistent with its primary purposes. The way the congregation performs its ministry and fulfills its mission may be a better revelation of its true beliefs than official words in some formal document. The theology a congregation acts upon is more important than a theology it votes upon. The plea here is that the two ought to be interlocked.

A congregation, under the guidance of the Holy Spirit and the best instruction available, should frame its beliefs as related to God, the church, and the world. If those beliefs are valid and theologically defensible, they should serve as the foundation upon which that congregation continues to function. Such commitment not only provides direction but also motivation. When a congregation believes that it is functioning in accordance with the will of God and is the recipient of his blessing, this conviction is the source of even further power.

This truth is revealed beautifully in a concluding statement made in a book commemorating the fiftieth anniversary of the Allen Temple Baptist Church. "The first fifty years . . . have been years of triumph in the midst of trials, testings, and transitions."[9] The concluding comment declares, "Within the congregation is the deep conviction that the church . . . has come 'thus far by faith, leaning on the Lord.'"

Appropriately, words from the gospel song greatly loved by the congregation were used as the title to the book of history: *Thus Far by Faith*. That conviction is a true source of power!

NOTES

1. See R. W. Kicklighter, "The Origin of the Church," *What Is the Church?* ed. Duke K. McCall (Nashville: Broadman Press, 1958), pp. 28-45.

2. William Barclay, *New Testament Words* (Philadelphia: The Westminster Press, 1974), pp. 68-72. K. L. Schmidt, "Ekklesia," *Theological Dictionary of the New Testament*, ed. Gerhard Kittel, trans. and ed. Geoffrey W. Bromiley (Grand Rapids: Wm. B. Eerdmans Publishing Co., 1962), vol. III, pp. 501-536.

3. Barclay, p. 174.

4. Theron D. Price, "Church," *Encyclopedia of Southern Baptists* (Nashville: Broadman Press, 1958), Vol. I, pp. 272-76.

5. Dale Moody, *The Word of Truth* (Grand Rapids: William B. Eerdmans Publishing Company, 1981), p. 427.

6. Unpublished papers describing the work of Allen Temple Baptist Church will be identified by name but will not be cited in reference notes. They are available only through the church.

7. J. Alfred Smith, "Undergirding the Church's Mission," *The Church in Bold Mission* (Atlanta: Home Mission Board, SBC, 1977), pp. 159-160.

8. Smith, p. 160.

9. J. Alfred Smith, *Thus Far by Faith* (Oakland, CA: Color Art Press, 1973), p. 69.

3/Establishing Congregational Identity

It already has been noted that a congregation which functions as the visible church in a given locality has both an inward and an outward relationship. How can that collection of human beings become a unified whole, function as the "body of Christ," and experience fellowship in a manner that will prove mutually supportive? And then how can that same group turn its attention outward so as to be effective in witnessing to the glory of God and the lordship of Christ in the community and world? There are no simple and easy answers to these questions, and this entire book is an effort to discover multiple approaches. This chapter provides emphasis upon the importance of the congregation giving attention to its own identity. A sense of accurate self-awareness is directly related to a congregation's ability to build and preserve fellowship. It seems equally true that being in touch with its nature and diversity may enable a congregation to know how to project its ministry to the community and world in a more productive manner.

Internal Christian fellowship within a group, especially of the type worthy to be called *koinonia*, does not occur among strangers. While the tie that binds Christians together is Christ himself and the common belief in him, the more persons know and understand each other, the more they will be sensitive to each other's needs. Personal encouragement and support can be more easily extended

41

and received among persons who are aware of needs, strengths, and weaknesses of each other. To know and be known is an asset in developing the deepest sense of caring.

A congregation always finds it helpful to be aware of its internal strengths and limitations as it determines how to deploy its resources in ministry. Perception of the tie to heritage, the common core of theological beliefs, the diversity and extent of talents, and the degree of commitment to its recognized mission are all facets that will have a bearing upon the efforts of a congregation to relate itself to the world.

It seems, therefore, that there are good theological and psychological reasons for contending that a congregation needs to establish clearly its own sense of identity. Who are we as a congregation? From where have we come? How are we now constituted as a collection of people? What are we trying to do together? What are our strengths, capabilities, and goals? These are but a few of the questions we need to answer as we expand our self-awareness.

In Terms of History

Following graduation from the seminary, I was preparing to move to a pastorate in another state. In the days before arriving there I had the opportunity to read a written history of that particular church. What seemed like a faraway and relatively unknown congregation suddenly became real. Here was a church with a heritage. Many of the present members had strong ties with the past, and I was able to get in touch with the foundations upon which they were continuing to build. It would be easier to understand some of their traditions and why some of them held such deep convictions about certain aspects of their work. This written document was a most significant finding, and I was happy to become a history student again.

Not many days after arriving in that community as pastor, I sat one afternoon on a front porch and talked with an elderly gentleman about his long experience in the community and church. He pointed to a huge tree in the yard and told me how he remembered bending it over and topping it with a pocket knife. All his life he had lived in that place, and through all those years he had been closely tied to the church. His oral history served to illumine the written history I had explored already. When I completed that visit, I felt more a part of the church and more in touch with its past.

How important it is to become familiar with the beginnings and continuity of a congregation if one is to feel a sense of belonging. New pastors need to make the discovery, and they need to teach that heritage to other newcomers.

Let us look, as an illustration, at the Allen Temple Baptist Church. This church was established in 1919 in the eastern portion of the city of Oakland, California. The dominant population of East Oakland at that time was comprised of Portuguese and other middle-income, non-black Baptists. Most of the black population lived in West Oakland. The new Northern Baptist congregation would serve initially a small number of black Baptists. The recorded history gives an account of both the changes in the city and in congregation dating from 1919. It traces the development of the church in terms of its membership makeup, growth of facilities, the highlights of ministry under seven pastors, and how the church reached the level of its operation in 1973—the date of the written history *Thus Far by Faith*. Other written historical documents treat the years since 1973.[1]

This is not the place to record the history of Allen

Temple, nor even to provide an extensive summary of what has been written already. The emphasis here is to report that the members of this congregation are aware of their history and feel themselves a part of it. They know from where they have come and how they got to where they are. They believe in their heritage and find occasions to celebrate it and add to it. This is healthy for the congregation. Roots are very important, and Allen Temple people neither ignore nor deny them.

The written history of Allen Temple speaks of "Humble Birth," "Struggle for Survival," "Achievement of Stability," "Healing and Reconciliation" which followed a division in 1950 with another congregation emerging, and the concluding section on "New Beginnings." Other documents recount the progress made in recent years, but none as well as the annual reports presented to the church by the pastor and various leaders of programs and committees.

It is valuable for this kind of history to be recorded and for written documents to be preserved and treasured. A danger exists only if a people become slaves to the past and bound by it. If it serves to shackle them, to rob them of new aspirations, then the stress upon heritage becomes nonproductive. But if it serves as incentive and as instruction as intended, heritage is a blessing.

A college professor once addressed a group of male students, "Young men, standing upon your father's shoulders, you ought to be able to see farther and reach higher than they." And so we ought also in the congregational context.

There are many good sources which will help congregations study their histories. Many denominations provide workbooks which suggest certain data to compile.[2] Usually they encourage recording factual data related to origin, property and building developments across the years, changes in leadership, noting any missions or new churches which may have come from the congregation, factors which may help understand either growth or decline in the membership, and other highlights. If this material is to be used as a part of church planning for the future, there will usually be a section which helps the user reflect upon the history and see implications for the future. Many congregations, having made such a historical study, have been known to publish either a longer history as a book or a permanent brochure which can be distributed to members and treasured for years.

In Terms of Place

In recent years the importance of the social setting for a congregation's ministry has been appropriately identified and stressed. It is a fact that the fastest growing churches in America tend to be urban. Further documentation demonstrates that where a church is located within a city in terms of facility and ministry greatly influences its growth or decline in membership. As far back as 1935 H. Paul Douglass, highly renowned for his church and community studies, pointed out a characteristic of urban churches:

> Where the environment is prosperous and progressive the church can scarcely fail to "succeed." Where it is miserable and deteriorating the church can scarcely avoid failure.
> The most crucial of the environmental facts is that modern social changes are so many and so great and that they come so fast as to put unparalleled stress upon the church today.[3]

Fifty years later sees no change in this phenomenon, at least as a general rule. Much has been written about the community contextual factors and their impact upon a local church.[4] Especially has this been examined as related to the community in transition. If an urban community has been undergoing a loss of population or a considerable change in the racial and/or economic characteristics related to the population, the churches of that community are likely to experience a decline in membership or at least no further growth. Rare exceptions to this general rule are sometimes found.

Because of the social factors which impinge upon the church and its ministry, it has become common to characterize communities and churches as types. Ezra Earl Jones has developed a typology used by many.[5] He specifies six types: (1) Downtown, (2) Neighborhood, (3) Metropolitan-Regional, (4) Special Purpose, (5) Small Town, and (6) Open Country. It will be noted that five of these are related to geography, but that the Special Purpose Type could be located anywhere. Lyle Schaller has developed a typology that combines both geographic and social features in his book *Hey, That's Our Church!*[6] For the most part, Schaller places more emphasis upon psychological or attitudinal characteristics and tends to de-emphasize geographic components. In another book Schaller uses a typology based upon size and age, and this also would stress the importance of psychological and attitudinal characteristics of membership.[7]

For my own treatment of church and community typology I tend to stay with a strict geographic emphasis.[8] Moving from the center core of the city outward there seem to be five geographic types: (1) Downtown, (2) Inner City or Transitional, (3) Stable, (4) Suburban, and (5) Rural-Urban Fringe. The Downtown generally is where the "Old First" church is found, unless it has relocated. The Inner City or Transitional is that section of the city that by virtue of age has undergone physical deterioration and may be occupied by persons in the lower income level and of varied races. The Stable Community is the territory of both residences and businesses that are well established, not yet facing significant deterioration, and there is little undeveloped land so that new developments are not very likely. The Suburban Community lies at the edge of the city and continues to expand in territory and grow in population. The Rural-Urban Fringe is that community located between the suburb and the open country, where both city and country meet and merge.

A congregation may not know what type it is in terms of culture or psychology, but it should be able to identify its type geographically. Once that is done, the pastor and other leaders can then study the characteristics of that sociological type and move from generalizations about it to the specifics of the particular congregation. It is obvious that the churches in these five geographic-type communities do differ, even as the people who live in them differ.

To supplement the typology based on geography, one needs to distinguish between churches that tend to be neighborhood type in membership and those that tend to draw members from across community lines, even to the point of being metropolitan in scope.

Another typology of considerable value is the one that Anderson and Jones treat under their discussion of the "Stages in the Life Cycle of a Community."[9] The five types are of a developmental nature and are listed as: (1) the newly developing community, (2) stable community, (3) pretransitional communities, (4) transitional communities, and (5) posttransitional communities. These types are influenced by what is happening in a particular territory as a result of aging, mobility, racial, and economic change, and other factors which may alter the landscape and the people who reside there.

These ways of characterizing communities in their developmental movements can be helpful as an overlay upon the geographic types. A downtown community, for example, may be stable, pretransitional, transitional, or post-transitional. In each case it may still continue to be "downtown." In contrast, a "stable" community ceases to be stable once it becomes pretransitional or transitional, but it may return to being stable when it becomes post-transitional. Typology, therefore, is simply a valuable way of thinking about community as place. Once identified and described, it enables church leadership to understand more fully some of the characteristics of the community that will influence either the growth or decline of the congregation and the opportunities and limitations of its potential ministry.

Working with Allen Temple Church as a model, let us note that the immediate community in which the facilities are located is inner-city or transitional. Deterioration of both residences and businesses exist within a few blocks of the church building, although much stability also can be found. This combination is what characterizes the community as transitional. However, Allen Temple is not the typical church in a transitional community. The church, in terms of type, has become metropolitan-regional, drawing members from far outside the immediate community. Except for this expansion, the church could well be in a state of decline. Instead, remarkable growth continues monthly, a fact related to the church's awareness of where it is and its unique opportunities for ministry.

For Allen Temple, therefore, it is important for us to understand both the immediate community which is a focus of its ministry and the larger community from which the church draws members and contributes its influence.

In Terms of Membership

The racial components of a particular community which a church considers its place of ministry normally should be represented within the congregation. In many urban

neighborhoods the population for the most part is composed predominantly of only one race, and this racial
composition is the predominant membership of the local
church. However, where urban pluralism crosses racial
and ethnic lines, it should become possible for the church
to reflect this new pluralism also. No church should plan
its ministry with the intention of a restricted membership.
The "homogeneous principle" has been stressed greatly in
recent years,[10] and there is truth within it worth exploring.
It seems theologically invalid, however, to be content with
a homogeneous church if there are persons within the
immediate community who are not a part of any congregation. The Christian church today must never subscribe to
the theory that "if they are not like us they cannot be a part
of us." This is not to imply that culture is unimportant. The
church that hopes to become multiethnic/racial will soon
recognize the difficulty with which it is faced.[11] Usually an
integrated membership is accomplished more easily in the
larger congregation which may have become metropolitan-
regional in its scope, and even then there likely will be one
race that will be predominant within the membership.

The community surrounding the Allen Temple Church,
predominantly white in earlier years, is now 90 percent
black. As would be expected, therefore, the church's
membership is predominantly black, but the church is
careful to stress that it wishes to be of service to everyone,
regardless of race, age, economics, or culture. Five different racial/ethnic groups are represented in the church
membership: Black, white, American Indian, Chinese,
and Mexican American. Members represent all types of
life-styles and interests. They come from all parts of the
city. Included among them are the highly trained professionals, the manual laborers, the elderly and retired,
university students, younger children, and other persons
representing the components of the general population.

This wide variety reflects the fact that the congregation draws members from outside the immediate community.

Some categories of membership arranged by social characteristics may help to show the nature of Allen Temple, while at the same time indicating one way a congregation should study itself if it wishes to understand its social makeup. Table 1 indicates the distribution of membership by place of residence.

Table 1
Membership by Residences

Zip Code	Percent
94605	27.7
94603	17.3
94621	14.6
94601	5.4
94619	5.4
15 other zip codes	
within city	14.0
outside city limit	15.6

The Allen Temple Church is located within zip code 94621, but some of the people who live in zip codes 94605 and 94603 are closer to the building than some on the fringes of zip code 94621. By count, 70.4 percent of the members live within four miles of the building. It is estimated that of the other members, about 15 percent live within 4-12 miles, 8 percent between 12-20 miles, and about 7 percent more than 20 miles from the church building. Some families are known to come regularly from 35 miles away.

When persons come from some distance to participate within a congregation, this indicates a sense of great loyalty and of personal fulfillment. Sometimes such loyalty was developed when the members resided closer to the church neighborhood and is maintained in spite of the distance now experienced. Any church faced with this type of situation must be careful to sustain the membership in the more distant places if the loyalty and participation are to continue. Where there is a belief in what the church is doing and a commitment to the ministry, persons may want to continue to be a part of it. For example, one person at Allen Temple, a professional who lives outside the city, expressed it this way: "When one joins this church, he is put to work. They ask who you are and what can you do? And then they give you a job. Working in the church makes my faith grow." This person did not have to live in the neighborhood to feel that he was a part of the church. The satisfactions he received from his participation kept him coming.

Table 2
Membership by Age

Age	Percent
0-19	15.2
20-29	17.6
30-39	19.5
40-49	19.2
50-59	19.0
60-69	8.2
70-up	1.5
Median Age 37	
Average Age 40	

A study of age distribution among a church's membership will show if the church generally is reaching all groups within the population of the community. It also will indicate something of the promise of the church for the future. In the case of Allen Temple, as indicated in

Table 2, it appears that all age groups are well represented. Age distribution of Oakland as recorded in the 1980 census is not available at this time. When comparisons are made later when that data becomes available, it may show that the church does not reach as many persons over sixty as would be expected, even though the black population over sixty is not large. The church does have strong appeal for younger adults at this time, and that seems clearly indicated by the data. The median age of membership is higher than for the population as a whole, but this is explained by the absence of younger children being counted in church membership. These are included in the Sunday School and are very prominent in the life of the church. With as many youth and young adults involved, the future of the church looks bright.

Any church which makes a study of this type will discover where additional emphasis may need to be given in its ministry and outreach. It may also have cause for satisfaction or of concern as it projects what ten to twenty years may bring.

Table 3
Membership by Education

Highest Education Level Attained	Percent
Grades 1-6	2.3
Grades 7-10	5.0
Grades 11-12	24.0
College 1-3 years	34.6
College/University 4-6 years	28.1
College/University 7 + years	6.0

A table like Table 3 does not always aid one in determining the educational level of adults. Given the fact that 15.2

percent of the membership is under twenty years of age and the fact that 31.3 percent of the membership has acquired no more than a high school education, it can be concluded that several adults have terminated their education with high school graduation, or less. The remarkable thing about Allen Temple's membership is the high percentage (68.7) who have been to college, with 34.1 percent having graduated and many doing graduate study after the initial degree. This accounts for the leadership level seen in the congregation, and for the larger than average number of professional people being active.

A church needs to know this kind of information if activities and programs are to be developed which will address the needs, interests, and abilities of the people.

Table 4
Membership by Income

Annual Income Range	Percent
$ 0.00- 1,999	9.9
2,000- 4,999	4.1
5,000- 6,999	3.8
7,000- 9,999	4.8
10,000-11,999	5.4
12,000-14,999	10.8
15,000-19,999	18.7
20,000-24,999	16.9
25,000-29,999	8.2
30,000-34,999	6.5
35,000-39,999	5.7
40,000-49,999	2.3
50,000-up	2.9

The information in Table 4 indicates that the median income range at Allen Temple falls between $15,000-

$19,999, which means that the congregation as a whole would be classified as comfortable but not in the higher range of income. However, with 25.4 percent recorded as being at the $30,000 and above level of income, the congregation has the potential to maintain an adequate financial base for a progressive program. The high percentage of persons in the lower income levels provides the church the opportunity to bring encouragement, care, and sometimes direct assistance to persons who live on a submarginal level.

Every church needs to give attention to the financial conditions of its membership. People may be found who are in need and desire to be assisted financially. A study of the records also will reveal something of the stewardship capabilities of the members.

Table 5
Membership by Marital Status

Category	Percent
Single	36
Married	43
Widowed	5
Separated/Divorced	16

Table 5 is based on a random sample of 100 persons over 18 years of age. It may not be totally representative of all adults within the membership. Within the sample, 70 percent were female, 30 percent male.

The above data, reinforced by observation and interviews, reveals that the Allen Temple Church has a rather high percentage of single adults. For these persons the church provides a source for personal interaction and association. Single adults, especially the widowed, separated, and divorced, need to belong to a group in which they can experience acceptance and support. Information of the type in Table 5 shows a congregation how much its ministry is needed, and it points out some of the possible dimensions for that ministry.

Census data on households and families, when compiled and analyzed, can serve as a valuable source for church leadership. While internal church studies can sensitize leadership to the needs of members, expanded community data can reveal the extent of family needs in the larger social context.

Beyond the data set forth in the above tables, there is some further information related to the Allen Temple membership which is useful for a church to have. For example, there are over 1100 families included in the membership of Allen Temple. The average size family has 3.12 members, and this provides opportunity for some family-type ministry.

The membership is composed of members who have belonged to the church for many years, but also a large number who have joined in very recent years. While the average length of membership is 8.08 years, new members are being added at such a rate as to indicate that the median length of membership is soon going to be much less than it is now. This highlights the importance of the assimilation of new members within the membership, a concern shared by many churches fortunate enough to be experiencing rapid growth.

The self-perceptions of a congregation are important. In response to a questionnaire, the Allen Temple membership, based upon a random sample, made several interesting responses.

In terms of how they felt about their relationship to the church, 65 percent declared they "always" felt they were a vital part of the church, 25 percent said they "usually" or "sometimes" felt that they were, and only 10 percent declared that they did not feel like they were "a vital part of the church." Without having a basis for comparison, I do not know the significance of these figures, but I think that it might indicate a higher level of fellowship than would be experienced by many congregations.

Most members rightly perceive their church to be large, to be economically middle class, and to maintain an open policy of acceptance of all persons. A large majority (81 percent) thought that in time of trouble the church would provide assistance. Another 15 percent felt this assistance might be given depending upon the situation. Only 4 percent had doubt about such assistance being given. Again, these figures would indicate a high concept of fellowship.

Any congregation might find it highly enlightening to learn of the self-perception of members, especially when they can answer anonymously. Such surveys from time to time could help a church evaluate the degree of fellowship achieved by the congregation.

In Terms of Programs

Most church consultants want a congregation to secure the data that will enable an historical analysis of church activities, programs, and services to be made. Denominational guidebooks contain forms on which such data may be compiled.[12] These usually suggest recorded numerical data of enrollment, attendance, and participation in various organizations, such as Sunday School. To see what have been the actual numbers over a period of years, usually ten to twenty, will enable trends to be determined.

In addition to any statistical studies made of participants in organizations, it is also useful to allow members to express their views about the effectiveness of these organizations. Table 6 shows the response of Allen Temple members to such an opportunity. The data is based upon a

Table 6
Membership Satisfaction Levels with Programs or Activities
(By number of responses of sample)

Program/Activity	Very Satisfied	Satis-fied	Dissat-isfied	Very Dis-satisfied
Worship Services	73	25		
Prayer Meeting/Bible Class	66	14	1	
Sunday Church School	63	20	2	
Women's Activities	23	36	8	
Men's Activities	16	26	14	
Youth Activities	20	26	10	2
Children's Activities	26	29	10	1
Leadership Development	39	25	6	
Christian Social Concerns	35	26	4	
Athletics	18	31	7	
Music Ministry	52	21	4	1
Deacon Board	35	22	7	
Deaconess Board	30	29	3	2
Trustees	31	24	5	
Evangelism Efforts	35	27	6	
Stewardship Emphasis	24	30	6	
Community Outreach	49	28	4	
Facilities	51	17	3	
Welcome of Visitors	66	22	1	
Missionary Emphasis	42	32	1	

random sample of knowledgeable persons, representing members who had belonged for less than a year to more than twenty years. Not all answered in regard to each program, but they tended to respond to the programs in which they had some basis for a valid judgement.

While a form like Table 6 is not as complete or useful as a total survey of the entire congregation might be, it is adequate to indicate the greater strengths and limitations in the programs. The data could serve to alert leadership to take another look at these areas where dissatisfaction exists. A more complete investigation could then determine areas for improvement or change.

Should a church discover that statistics documented growth or continued interest in a program, and the respondents indicated satisfaction, this would suggest reasonable effectiveness. However, if either or both measurements raised questions, it may be assumed that attention ought to be given to that program.

Table 6 serves to identify the full scope of programs at Allen Temple. Some of these will be discussed more fully in other chapters.

In Terms of Facilities

At intervals a congregation ought to study the use it is making of its building and grounds. Recently, I visited a church where the leadership knew that the Sunday School organization needed to be expanded, but they felt this could not be done until further building could occur. A careful study of how they were using their present facilities revealed that with some reordering of use they could find space for four more Sunday School classes immediately. Sometimes a functional approach to building use can indicate a way to secure space and efficiency for the organization.

At Allen Temple Church one can observe building

expansion over the years simply by walking around the block and looking at new wings or buildings that have been added at five different times since the first building was placed on the current lot. The latest building to be completed was entered in October, 1981. This building provides a new sanctuary, all church offices, choir rooms, and some other rooms for classes, conferences, or special activities. At this writing, the congregation is in the process of renovating the former sanctuary and converting it into educational space. As growth occurs, this church continues to build and to acquire new property when lots become available. They have also made use of public school property and grounds which are nearby.

In most growing churches, a continuous study needs to be made of how best to use existing facilities and how to plan for additional buildings by the time it is needed. Feasibility studies, such as Allen Temple made in 1977, are absolutely essential in order to secure adequate facilities of the right kind and in order to make sure that a congregation does not overbuild. I have visited churches which were still paying for property that already had ceased to be used because the projected growth rate was not experienced. The rule is that careful and accurate planning must occur before any expansion of facilities is pursued.

In Terms of Stewardship Capability

Most congregations have little idea of the true financial potential of the total membership. Planning all too frequently is based upon the previous year's budget or giving, with not even an acceptable challenge goal. Also, records of contributions may not be kept accurately, and if kept may not be shared adequately. Individual contributions should always be confidential information. However, some summation of a congregation's giving habits may be shared in a manner that will be informative and serve as an incentive. Some churches compile such records by family giving patterns, such as reporting all families who are reported to have given nothing during a year and then the number of families reported in each of escalating contribution brackets. For example, if the family income levels are reported as was true in Table 4 above, contribution brackets revealing giving habits could document faithfulness in stewardship or lack of it. One church noted that 20 percent of the families gave 80 percent of the church offerings, a fact in that church indicating considerable potential for improvement in giving. The need for stewardship education became apparent, as did the need for more adequate budget promotion and more effort at proper motivation for giving.

Allen Temple Church records are not compiled and shared in the manner discussed above. However, total giving records for the congregation are shared and compared to previous years, as indicated in a graph and table they have printed for their use.

Table 7
Giving Records for Allen Temple

Year	Offerings	Building Fund
1977	$245,825	—
1978	374,335	$113,000
1979	469,355	138,650
1980	521,023	150,000
1981	575,732	166,000

The graph, of course, showed the escalating contributions each of the past five years and was compiled both by years and by months within the years. This provided a visual presentation for the people to view progress month by month. It is not surprising to observe that giving is smaller during the summer months, as was also true of attendance. The high month generally was October.

Implication for Church Planning

Not all aspects for church concern have been treated within this chapter. Some have been reserved for later chapters where they can receive a more specialized presentation. Enough has been included here to indicate the importance for the leadership of a church to gather data about congregational identification and to share it with the members.

The theory which has been proved to be sound is that a congregation that understands itself is more able to preserve its fellowship and organize itself for the work it needs to be doing. The kind of studies suggested above are helpful to indicate strengths and areas of need. Strengths must be used to maximum advantage. Needs will not be met simply with the passing of time. Intelligent planning enables a group to know how to approach needs most effectively. Such planning cannot be pursued apart from gathering all information which can be used as an asset in planning. These are the reasons that denominational agencies provide materials and consultation to enable churches to act with intentionality.

In 1977, the Allen Temple Baptist Church, with some assistance from the American Baptist Convention, made the most comprehensive study of its church and community that had been made up to that time. This study served to show the way for improvement of church organizations, but also was used as a study to determine the needs for building and the potentials for the immediate future. I do not think that the remarkable progress this church has made during the last five years was accidental. It occurred because of the commitments and planning of pastor, leaders, and congregation. As a result, the church has more confidence in itself. It is now committed to the planning process. Especially does it seem to be committed to an intensified ministry within its community and city. Inasmuch as the church has implemented the approaches discussed within this chapter, it serves as a model for examination.

NOTES

1. J. Alfred Smith, "Allen Temple Baptist Church, Oakland, California," *Models of Metropolitan Ministry*, compiler B. Carlisle Driggers (Nashville: Broadman Press, 1979), pp. 79-84; "Church History," *New Building Dedication, Allen Temple Baptist Church, 1981.*

2. *Church and Community Survey Workbook* (Nashville: Convention Press, 1970).

3. H. Paul Douglass, *The Protestant Church as a Social Institution* (New York: Russell and Russell, 1935), pp. 237-238.

4. Dean R. Hoge and David A. Roozen, *Understanding Church Growth and Decline, 1950-1978* (New York: The Pilgrim Press, 1979). For an application of this concept to a case analysis, see C. Kirk Hadaway, "The Demographic Environment and Church Membership Change," *Journal for the Scientific Study of Religion.* 20 (1): 77-89.

5. Ezra Earl Jones, *Strategies for New Churches* (New York: Harper and Row, Publishers, 1976), pp. 35-42.

6. Lyle E. Schaller, *Hey, That's Our Church!* (Nashville: Abingdon Press, 1975).

7. Lyle E. Schaller, *The Passive Church* (Nashville: Abingdon Press, 1981).

8. An older treatment similar to this may be found in Murray H. Leiffer, *The Effective City Church* (Nashville: Abingdon Press, 1961).

9. James D. Anderson and Ezra Earl Jones, *The Management of Ministry* (New York: Harper and Row, Publishers, 1978), pp. 37-42.

10. See literature in the field of church growth studies, especially Donald McGavran and Win Arn, *How To Grow a Church* (Glendale, CA: Regal Books, 1973); Hoge and Roozen, *Understanding Church Growth and Decline, 1950-1978;* "Evangelism and Church Growth," *Review and Expositor,* LXXVII, No. 4, Fall, 1980; Martin E. Marty, "Is the Homogeneous Unit Principle of Church Growth Christian?" *Context* (March 15, 1978), p. 3.

11. Walter E. Ziegenhals, *Urban Churches in Transition* (New York: The Pilgrim Press, 1978).

12. *Church and Community Survey Workbook;* Jere Allen and George Bullard, *Shaping a Future for the Church in the Changing Community* (Atlanta: Home Mission Board, SBC, 1981).

4/Discovering Ministry Possibilities Beyond the Congregation

Previous emphases upon theology have enforced the conviction that every church must be committed to ministry, not to its own members alone but to those beyond the congregation. Mission and ministry are the primary purposes for being. They are to be related to a church's statement of purpose, and they should be derived from the objectives which have been identified by a congregation.

The term *ministry* as used here refers to the efforts of a church, through both its professional staff and lay membership, to extend its witness and service to those who are not its own members. In reality, the church may be ministering unto itself while attempting to minister unto others, for the witness grows through witnessing, and the one engaged in service finds his or her own life greatly enriched. The church's ministry belongs to all the people of God, not to be confined to the recognized "ordained" ministers.

For about twenty years at least, local congregations, denominations, and interfaith groups have been accelerating the search for new forms of ministry. Renewal efforts have been made to reexamine the ministry of the church in the light of the ministry of Jesus and his instruction to the church. The theology of servanthood has been recovered. More and more Christians are coming to recognize that every human concern is a concern of God and ought to become a concern for his church. Spurred on by this theology, the church has expanded its ministry to engulf a much larger segment of life and to find ways of relating redemptively in the world to persons and groups too long neglected.

New forms of ministry today are found at almost every level of church involvement.[1] These forms are used to enhance worship, as in the use of drama, music, and other art forms. Those who come into the sanctuary are blessed, but the new forms make it possible to take the message into the world: to shopping centers, resort areas, city parks, and wherever a possible hearing might be achieved.

Other ministry forms may find the congregation using the professional skills of laypersons in ways unthought of a generation ago. Carpenters go to a mission field to help construct a building. Doctors provide a health clinic in a neglected section of the city. Professional persons serve as tutors to troubled children who need assistance with difficult subjects. Lawyers take the case of clients unable to pay for the service. Youth engage in a cleanup, paint-up campaign in a rundown area. No need is considered out-of-bounds for imaginative Christians who are seeking to "join Christ in ministry in the world."

Again it must be seen that the most effective outreach ministry is not likely to occur without planning. While spontaneous ministries may spring up without advance planning, and should be welcomed and encouraged, ministries that are to continue usually will have to be based on careful survey and preparation. Responsible leadership will insist upon a design for church ministry that is flexible and that is related to human needs. Both the deification of the status quo and of innovation must be avoided as the church searches for new "wineskins" for the gospel.

It should be perfectly obvious that a church will want to care for its own. Unless it does good to those who are "of the household of faith," it will have neglected the biblical mandate. The previous chapter helped us see how to identify the needs of the congregation. This chapter will explore how a congregation determines opportunities for ministry in the larger community of which it is a part. Through praying, giving, and sending, the church may be able to reach to the ends of the earth. It will want to engage in this witness in whatever way possible. Within the community and city where members of the congregation reside, however, there is a special opportunity for ministry. Praying, giving, and sending may be important here too, but even more personal involvement is possible. This is the arena in which people live out their daily lives. They serve, bless, love, hate, hurt, help each other every day. They ignore and pass by, and they seek out and serve. As Christians they need to search for ways to maximize their influence. This suggests the importance of making some discoveries about the nature of the community and the needs to be found within it.

Why Study the Community?

Many persons study the community to get answers to the personal concerns and interests that they have. Parents may be concerned about the impact of the community upon their children. The city councilman may be concerned about the shrinking tax base and what will happen if the city continues to decline. The policeman's concern is related to crime, where it will strike next and maybe his own safety. Educators wonder about changes in the values they detect and what this means for the support of education. A minority group may be concerned about what it perceives as grave social injustice. There may indeed be as many personal reasons for studying the community as there are special groups or causes.

Maybe these varied concerns can be caught up in the more systematic reasons for studying a community as defined by a social scientist. Indeed his reasons for studying a community are the same ones a church would use. He studies the community because he finds within it a comprehensive social universe.[2] The wholeness of life is seen in community. The community is larger than persons, but it contains the story of persons and their interactions with one another. It is larger than families, but within it families secure their stability or experience their disintegration. The community is larger than a racial group, but the group must find the quality of its life in the context of the community. A church must deal with all aspects of the social environment, an environment never understood by looking at isolated parts but at the whole of community.

The community is a social form that has characterized human life from the beginning. The community is the place wherein people achieve their sense of belonging, seek self-preservation, and search for true humanity and fulfillment. From a Christian perspective, human existence is intended to be lived in community and solidarity rather than in isolation and solitude.[3]

Church and community interrelate. The church cannot help but be influenced by what happens in the community. We would like to think that the relationship is reciprocal so that what happens within the church has impact upon the community. These, then, provide adequate motivation and reasons for studying the community. How will the church be influenced by the community, and how may the church provide a ministry within the community? Some study needs to be made.

How Study the Community?

The most revealing way to study a community is through observation. As a consultant with a church, one thing I always like to do immediately is to drive through the community under the guidance of someone who knows the territory generally perceived to be the "church community." To see the houses, stores, schools, church buildings, and general development begins to reveal a little of what life might be like. Are they well kept or deteriorating? Are streets and sidewalks in good repair and clean? Is there evidence that trash collection is neglected? And in addition to physical surroundings, what can one learn through observation about human values and needs? When the public school lets out in the afternoon, what happens to the students? Where do they go? What do they do? Is there evidence of the need for after-school activities of a supervised nature, especially for small children? Are idle adults seen on the street corners and in poolrooms and bars throughout the day? What kind of conversations are heard in barbershops, beauty shops, restaurants, and self-service laundries? Is there a means of public transportation? Are there playgrounds and parks in good use?

In terms of residential patterns, one can observe the proportion of single family dwellings to apartments and to public housing units. What size houses and of what value? Is there a wide distribution of residential types, from very expensive homes to ghettos?

The questions listed above are but a few that can be explored through careful observation, looking at the landscape and "behind" it. Many persons have not trained themselves to be observant and sensitive. Urban church specialists have made use of the "plunge" to introduce persons to the city and have used debriefing or theological reflection to help persons understand what they have seen and experienced. Some pastors have tried this approach in modified form by taking some of their church leadership on a walking field trip of several blocks surrounding their downtown or inner-city church buildings. The experiential way is an excellent method for getting a "feel" for the city and life within it.

Reconnaissance or observation can profitably be supplemented through the use of interviews. These may be both casual or structured. In Oakland, as part of my study of Allen Temple Church, I used both types. Eating alone in a diner, I had the chance to overhear conversations about the problems people were facing, or to ask questions of strangers with whom I had conversation. But in addition, I had numerous structured opportunities to talk with persons about their own life-styles, how long they had lived where they did, where they worked, their interests and aspirations. These conversations provided valuable insight as I began to get an idea about what life in East Oakland was like, and especially about the role the people allowed the church to take in helping them. With professional persons, my interviews were more highly structured through the use of specific questions. For example, I asked the mayor, a city councilman, the publisher of the major newspaper, a Catholic minister, a supervisor of the Parks and Recreation Department, and the executive of the Black United Fund this question: "What do you consider to be the major problems and needs of the city now and in the immediate future?" When I analyzed their answers I found that while they did not always rank the problems/needs in the same order, there was agreement that the list must include unemployment (especially among young blacks), crime, education, and housing. Even though I was a stranger to the city, I began to feel that I had a very accurate overview of life there and of some of the major concerns with which the city must grapple.

If one wants to understand a community, the interview can be used with much profit to research the concepts and opinions of leaders, average citizens, and persons who are the recipients of a particular service. It is a research tool which can aid one in gaining information, but also in determining attitudes. Sometimes it is very important to learn what views persons hold about aspects of life within the community. How deeply they hold their views may give some indication of the difficulty to be encountered in trying to bring about change. I know of no approach more useful in obtaining this kind of data than the interview. An earnest effort should be made to collect the data in a reliable manner, with objectivity and with as much freedom from bias as is possible. The pastor, or other religious leader, expecting to make extensive use of the interview as a research tool should become acquainted with some good social research material dealing with this topic.

Questionnaires can also be useful if an appropriate sample of the population can be obtained. Some churches have made use of them in mail outs to boxholders in a certain district, or by delivering them to doors personally and leaving a stamped envelope in which the questionnaire could be returned. This provides data of an anonymous nature, does not require conversation, and is a means of getting a larger number of responses than normally would be possible through personal interviews. I usually prefer to use interviews with selected leaders and questionnaires when a much larger sample is desired. No one should attempt to structure a questionnaire without securing assistance from research sources or specialists if there is any doubt regarding how to design the form. It must be clear as to the information requested, and it should be easy to answer, as is true of multiple choice responses.

The research approaches discussed above should be supplemented by studying the statistical and other factual data available through public sources. One might want to follow the guidance and forms available through denominational offices that deal with these kinds of studies.[4] In addition, guidance may be obtained by consulting social science-type sources such as Roland Warren, *Studying Your Community.*[5] Warren and other authorities help show how to make studies dealing with all of the major social systems within a community, such as the economy, government, education, health and welfare, the family, and organized religion. If any isolated area is to be studied, apart from the whole, assistance is available for that area only. These authorities help show how such studies are made, the kind of data available, and the type of questions one should use in order to cover adequately the area being researched.

One valuable source used extensively by church and denominational researchers to help determine the nature and needs of communities is the government census data. This source majors on demographic studies which help to characterize population groupings by geographic territories. The material can be of greatest use during the early years of each decade while the material is relatively current. It also serves the purpose of helping discover trends over many years, and it can be used to make projections for future years.

As an illustration of this type of study, let us apply it to California, to Oakland, and to the Allen Temple Church. The 1980 census showed that California was the number one state in total population gain between 1970-1980, an increase of 18.5 percent. Among the states, California was number 17 in white population gain, number two in gain of black population, but number one in population gain of American Indians, persons of Spanish origin, and persons

Table 8
Racial and Ethnic Composition
Oakland and East Oakland, 1980

Tracts	Total Population	Race					Spanish Origin
		Black	White	Asian and Pacific Islanders	American Indian, Eskimo, Aleut	Other Races	
All of Oakland	339,288	159,224 46.8%	129,690 38.2%	26,141 7.8%	2,199 0.7%	21,824 6.4%	32,491 9.6%
East Oakland only	149,966	85,574 57.1%	44,484 29.7%	8,247 5.5%	963 0.6%	10,698 7.1%	17,205 11.5%

of all "other" races. This was what had happened within the state and should have some influence upon the major metropolitan areas and the churches within them.

In Oakland, the population declined by 6 percent between 1940 and 1970, but the black population had grown considerably. For example in 1940, the nonwhite population in Oakland was less than 5 percent of the whole, but in 1970 it was 41 percent. By 1980 further change had occurred, as noted in Table 8.

Table 8 reveals the further changes that have occurred since 1970. It shows that the trends continue toward the growth of the nonwhite population and that a higher proportion of blacks and persons of Spanish origin are located in East Oakland. Taking note of this, Allen Temple Church has begun closer association with Spanish-speaking ministries, as will be described in the next chapter.

Although all of the 1980 census material is not available for distribution and use at the time of this writing, it is expected that the leadership of the Allen Temple Church will compile and use it later, much as they did the 1970 data. In their records and studies used for planning, they selected data they felt had meaning for their situation. Their analysis pointed to the differences between population groupings by race. "Whites are on the whole older, have higher incomes, and have fewer children [than blacks]."[6] The median age of Oakland's whites in 1970 was 39.1 years, while that of blacks was 23.7 years. Twenty of every 100 whites were 65 or over in 1970, but only 6 of every 100 blacks were 65 or over. Such figures as these help explain the absence of older blacks in the congregation in the proportion which might be expected.

The leaders at Allen Temple used census figures related to the younger age levels to provide insight to the opportunities for church ministry in that area. They noted that among blacks two of every five persons were under 18 years of age as compared to one in five for whites. Also they discovered that there were 43 of every 100 white females beyond the childbearing age, while only 18 in every 100 black females had reached that age. It was concluded that in Oakland the median age for blacks and whites was sure to widen. This kind of data says much to a church about what to expect in its community in the future.

When the church leadership studied the economic data of the census, they found that in their city a large portion of the population was poor, young, and old unemployed. The city itself sustained one of the highest unemployment rates in the nation, and members of ethnic minorities formed a disproportionately large segment of the population. In the 1970s, it was found that only one white family in 11 was listed at or below the poverty level, while blacks had one in four and Spanish surnames one in five. In 1982 the mayor of Oakland estimated that among black youth 60 percent were unemployed.

This kind of data sensitized the church leadership to many of the challenges facing them and the hardships facing some residents of their community. An article in *The Oakland Tribune*, January 8, 1979, showed this concern:

The pastor of East Oakland's progressive and popular Allen Temple Baptist Church had a few things to say to Oakland's mayor and city council. In a letter that Dr. J. Alfred Smith, Sr. delivered personally to City Hall, he says,

> Dear Elected Officials: I am very deeply disenchanted with a seemingly passive posture on your part about the existing human misery and hurt in our city over unemployment and your silence over a lack of a respectable implementation of affirmative action to remedy years of past discriminations in Oakland city government.
>
> What cuts more painfully is your repeal of the employee license tax without proposing alternatives for maintaining a

budget that would prevent the dismissal of large numbers of city employees in a city where unemployment is already too high.

In my community, I see young men standing on street corners because of unemployment. Too many existing businesses do not employ us, yet you care more about them than you do about us.

I am sure you seldom see the pain and poverty because you don't live and work among us. Nor do you represent us.

This kind of sensitivity and effort has not been uncommon at Allen Temple, and more will be said about it later. The point being made in this chapter is the importance of studying the community, getting factual data, understanding the community situation, so that when the church chooses to plan a ministry or engage in a social action it can become well informed before speaking or acting.

The Allen Temple leaders looked at what was happening in their community and concluded regarding economy:

If population trends continue, Blacks will move into the majority and be of low income with many at or below the poverty level.

The low purchasing power of these groups (Blacks and persons of Spanish origin) combined would no doubt have a tremendous effect on the central district's desirability as a business location, its function, and its configuration.

Private groups as well as civic and religious planning groups must also take the foregoing into consideration in meeting the future needs of Oakland as a community.

Here was a church attempting to see the vital interconnection between church and community. It sought to be responsible in trying to help build a better community and to plan church ministry in full light of the situation discovered within its community.

The leaders of the church compiled a list of the 100 largest employers in the Oakland area, numbering from 150 to 24,000 employees. They keep their people informed of opportunities, and they establish contact with employers, especially maintaining close relations with the largest employers in the area, Kaiser Aluminum.

The church also exercises an active concern about education, and their research shows that they have been serious in trying to understand the situation. They study school enrollment, the proportion of racial distribution of students and teachers, and the general conditions found in the schools. One school-board member, himself a resident of the community but not a member at Allen Temple, described for me how the schools now were attempting to stress the basics, especially reading. He described what he called a paternalistic attitude of many well-intentioned white teachers toward black students. "They conclude," he said, "that they need more love." "Instead," said he, "they need to be taught how to read and write; they need discipline and a challenge." He said he had a goal for education in his city that education become year around, making better use of facilities, cutting administrative costs, and improving the content of the educational offering. The church looks to these kinds of concerns and responds in two ways. They maintain an active support program through their encouragement to the schools and through their tutorial programs for students. They also "loan" their pastor to public education by allowing him to run for election to the school board, an election which he won easily last year. Already his influence is being felt.

In the field of social welfare, the church once more has

done its homework. Their records show that they maintain a directory of social service agencies within the community and both make and receive referrals. The agencies especially useful to them have been the health agencies, child care, drug and alcohol abuse, counseling, vocational testing, and law enforcement. In addition, they learn of the economic assistance services through both government offering and private sources.

Their summary of social service concerns in the late 1970s included employment, dependency, education, housing, delinquency, food, and clothing. They concluded that in an earlier day, "The members looked to their Church and Church leadership for survival, rededication and reentry into a society that has no plan for their existence." After years of work, there seems to be more confidence and hope, although their realism still tells them that they face an unending battle. Their hope leads them to promise: "The Allen Temple Baptist Church will continue to attempt to meet the needs of its members and that of the surrounding community. The emphasis is on the total person, spiritual, physical, and psychological."

The community studies made by the Allen Temple leaders turned to organized religion. They listed 41 churches of 200 or more members within a two-mile radius of Allen Temple. They have these located by address and identified on a city map. They maintain a relationship with some of them in several cooperative efforts, as will be discussed later. Their pastor maintains ministerial ties with other pastors both personally and through organizations. In addition to the main line churches, there are numerous small storefront churches in the area. Most of these have bivocational ministers and contact with them is difficult to establish or maintain. Almost no contact with these seems to exist.

Discovering Resources Within the Community

While a congregation makes a study of its community to try to determine the needs that exist there, it can at the same time attempt to discover the resources which may be allies in the effort to bring relief to persons facing these needs. Usually the needs in any metropolitan area are of two types: the kind that is limited enough to be addressed by one congregation and the kind that is so expansive and continuing as to need the attention of a resource or resources that go well beyond the ability of any one congregation to supply. The first type will be identified and addressed as quickly as a congregation can deploy its own resources in ministry. Larger needs will point toward a more sustained and organized effort.

In looking at community needs, a congregation should try to distinguish between the two types of needs. It should examine the nature of the need, the extent of it, and the length of its duration. For example, if the need is met today, will it reoccur tomorrow? A church may supply a week's rent and some groceries for a family where the head of a household is unemployed, but that need reoccurs at the end of the week unless employment is found. Where the unemployment rate in a city is high, a need exists within the field of economy that goes beyond the ability of one congregation to meet effectively. Perhaps all religious groups need to work with the business community and government in trying to build an environment which is more conducive to taking whatever action may be appropriate as related to employment.

The same type of illustration could be fashioned in areas where the other social systems are concerned. Needs in the fields of housing, health, education, crime prevention, and other such social issues need to be addressed by the total community. The church will need to see itself as a

part of the helping team, providing support, encouragement, and assistance in any way reasonable. It is not
uncommon for a church, or for clusters of churches or
religious leaders, to speak to the community as a social
conscience which helps sensitize the community.
Churches may function as critics and prophets, but they
should always remember to be quick to praise and support
when a positive word can be spoken.

The survey the church conducts should lead it to
discover its allies. These may be other nearby community
churches, the denomination as a whole, or a city-wide
interfaith group. Allies may also be found among the
helping professions, especially those in the health, welfare, educational, and law enforcement fields. Discover
where these sources exist, who the leaders are, and what
each group is best able to contribute to efforts to build a
better community.

In specific ways, church leaders may find those services
to which they may refer individuals. A church's referral
ministry is exceedingly important. A ready file should be
maintained regarding assistance in areas of counseling,
welfare, legal aid, health care, and other general assistance. A pastor needs to be viewed as a professional friend
to the helpers of the community. If good contacts are
maintained, and information readily available, the people
can be valuable resources for referral. Of course, referral
should be a two-way street, and the church should stay
prepared to accept the referral of cases with which it is able
to provide assistance.

Sometimes there are public or private groups who may
be able to extend grants, services, or other forms of
economic assistance to a church or group of churches. In
recent years, many churches have entered into agree-
ments with governmental programs whereby meals to the

elderly, health assistance through clinics, or counseling have been dispensed from a church building. While some churches have been reluctant to join such efforts because of their concern over separation of church and state, others have felt that arrangements could be made which would not violate principles for which the church stood. Private groups such as the United Way, corporations, or even individuals also have been used by churches to underwrite programs the church might not otherwise be able to provide. Day care, summer camps, or special recreational or educational programs are but a few of the types that have been pursued in this manner. Again it is important that a church through its leadership stay alert to these opportunities and try to cultivate them.

The Allen Temple Baptist Church is a good example of a church which has collaborated with other religious and community groups in working for a better community. They have searched for ways of extending their ministry and of finding allies in government, business, education, and the religious community. The ways in which they have used the resources they discovered will become a part of chapter 5.

NOTES

1. "New Patterns of Ministry," *Review and Expositor,* LXVI, No. 2, Spring, 1969.

2. Irwin T. Sanders, *The Community,* 3rd ed. (New York: The Ronald Press Company, 1975).

3. G. Willis Bennett, "Christian Ethics and Community Action," *Issues in Christian Ethics,* ed. Paul D. Simmons (Nashville: Broadman Press, 1980), pp. 77-92.

4. *Church and Community Survey Workbook* (Nashville: Convention Press, 1970); Jere Allen and George Bullard, *Shaping a Future for the Church in the Changing Community* (Atlanta: Home Mission Board, SBC, 1981).

5. Roland L. Warren, *Studying Your Community* (New York: Russell Sage Foundation, 1955); Bert E. Swanson and Edith Swanson, *Discovering the Community* (New York: Irvington Publishers, Inc., 1977).

6. *Survey Report, 1977*, Allen Temple Baptist Church, Oakland, CA.

5/Engaging in Ministry

Moving from research to ministry is always crucial and exciting. Analysis and planning take time and are essential if a church is to engage in a productive and effective ministry. When the time for action arrives, however, new motivation springs to life.

A church with a solid theology of mission should possess a genuine commitment which will enable it to develop strategies that are truly oriented toward needs. The problem generally is that more needs are discovered than any one congregation can address quickly. This is the reason that most planning efforts establish both long- and short-term goals. For example, in the study and planning efforts of the Allen Temple Church which were described earlier, goals were established in 1977 which are still in the process of being realized. Two of the most notable involved the new building and the new housing development, both completed in 1981. Other goals involving specific ministries can be entered into more rapidly, but building goals require stages of decision making and fund raising before new facilities emerge.

Because multiple actions usually are planned, and these require a length of time, it is necessary for a congregation to determine priorities. What shall be the first step? What order or ranking of priorities shall be assigned?

Some people assume that once needs of congregation and community are identified that the priority for action is determined by the ranking of needs. This is seldom the case. The number one need may not be the top priority, and certainly not the need chosen to be addressed first. For example, the group involved in recommending the actions to be taken may agree regarding the top priority, but they may also know that the one they choose may not be the one which will readily be accepted by the church. They may also know that it is not one which can be dealt with immediately.

Note, then, that two factors must be considered in establishing priorities for ministry: the degree of interest on the part of the church and the possibility of realization in light of existing resources. If sufficient numbers of the congregation are not in an agreement upon the need and desire for a particular ministry, it will be best to postpone that ministry until motivation for it can be encouraged. A new ministry should not be initiated with halfhearted commitment and inadequate desire. To do so might mean lack of support and even the willingness of the people to see it fail.

On the other hand the desire might be adequate, but careful research might show that resources do not exist which will assure success in ministry. In that event, it is generally wise to delay that ministry for a period of time until further resources can be secured.

Priorities for ministry must be determined by finding a proper balance between need, resources, and interest. If the ministry requires facilities, finances, and trained personnel, all three must be available in adequate strength before the ministry can be begun.

A congregation, after a period of intensive church and community research, may discover several needs, all of which may be established as priorities for action. In this event, a time frame, or calendar, may need to be established so that too many new efforts will not be attempted in too short a period of time. This will call for a ranking of the new ministries, not necessarily in the order of importance but in the order in which each will be phased into the life of the church.

Careful planning will lead to a determination of the organizational structure required for effective action to be taken. Leaders will be secured, trained, and prepared for each new ministry. The delegation of responsibility will be established and the degree and method of accountability will be designated. Effective supervision and support, whether from the pastor, other professional staff person, or a lay volunteer should be secured. Church members should not be expected to engage in continuing ministry without having adequate guidance at appropriate stages of development.

Let us turn now to an analysis of several ministries currently in existence at the Allen Temple Baptist Church. Similar ministries exist in other congregations. These illustrations are used, however, to demonstrate the intentional effort of one congregation to address the needs discovered through research within its church and community. These varied ministries are grouped into seven areas which the congregation wishes to address. They do not encompass all that the church does. For example, activities of the traditional nature, such as Sunday School, prayer meeting, music ministry, and worship are not treated in this chapter. It is understood that all of these are essential and are weekly efforts. The ministries addressed here are those designed to speak to particular needs, either in the congregation, community, or both.

In his preaching, teaching, and example Pastor Smith places continued stress upon the servant role of the church. He says, "Jesus gives you not a title but a towel."

He urges his people to remember:

> The world is where the mission of the local church must take place; this world of hurt where healing is needed; this world where hope is needed; this world where the scales of justice must be balanced; this world where sexism, racism, classism, and all 'evil-isms' strive to destroy human life; this is the world God loves and it is the place of mission for the local church.

The pastor is careful to point out that the ministry of the church is one all the people ought to pursue. Members are expected and trained to be active. Indeed, many of the ministries came into existence because of the interest of some members and their desire to get involved in doing something no one else was doing. This kind of commitment has made Allen Temple a seven-day-a-week church, both day and night. Activities in the church facilities, on public school property, in community centers and public playgrounds, in institutions, in the homes of members, and even on the streets occur every week. A description of several of these will be useful.

Relating to Needs in Education

The pastor and members of Allen Temple Church place consistent emphasis upon all forms of education. They stress quality in the work that they try to do. They plan for and give general support to public school education, adult education, colleges and universities, and to other forms of educational efforts. In addition, they try to maintain an environment which places high value on education and serves to encourage students and families to avail themselves of educational opportunities. The following examples will seem to bear out this claim.

Public School Education

In reviewing bulletins published throughout the year, one can find numerous references to public school education. These serve as announcements, recognitions, and appeals for support. Students are urged to take full advantage of their opportunities. Parents are encouraged to give support. Teacher-recognition days are observed, and the pastor and church use these to encourage the larger community to participate. On May 22, 1982, for example, the pastor had a "Letter to the Editor" published in *The Oakland Tribune*. It tells us much about his philosophy, commitment, and willingness to try to use his influence in the interest of education.

HONORING OAKLAND TEACHERS

If I trace the most important formative forces in my life, they would be family, church and public schools.

I am the kind of person that I am because of numerous teachers who loved me, counseled me, motivated me and had very high achievement expectations of me. They never allowed me to settle for less than the best. They taught me that true glory is *not* in never falling, but in rising every time.

My public school teachers followed my progress through college and graduate school, and the few who are still alive continue to communicate with me and my peers who are now in the adult world of vocations and citizenship.

Many competent, dedicated and underpaid persons who inspire children and youth are teachers in the Oakland public schools. They could have found new careers in better paying jobs and in less stressful environments than our overcrowded and underfunded public school classrooms.

On May 12 the Oakland Board of Education paid tribute to Oakland public school teachers by adopting a resolution acknowledging June 2 as Teachers Appreciation Day.

I salute our teachers and I join Superintendent J. David Bowick in urging all Oaklanders to observe Teachers Appreciation Day in whatever way they choose to honor the classroom heroines and heroes of our city.

J. ALFRED SMITH, SR.

Tutorial Program

This program, initiated several years ago by the pastor and principal of a neighborhood elementary school, has become a permanent fixture in the educational emphasis of Allen Temple Church. It was first designed to meet the needs of sixth grade boys and girls who were working one year below grade level. Assistance was given with homework, with special emphasis upon basic reading and mathematics. The students met with volunteer tutors on Tuesday and Thursday afternoons and on Saturday mornings.

The program became so successful that it was soon expanded and continues to receive strong support from the church. The last annual report showed an average afternoon attendance of 35 pupils working with seven tutors and five other volunteers, along with assistance of three adult staff members. High school students are used as tutors for younger children.

At the beginning of the fall term, the adult staff sponsors a training session for the new and continuing tutors. Workshops in developmental skills are scheduled at intervals. Parent workshops also are held. A leader from the

Division of Learning of the Oakland Public Schools provides instruction in the workshops.

Circles from the Women's Missionary Society provide supplies and refreshments daily. Special events of an enrichment nature are held.

The annual report specifies that the program has worked toward the goals of higher achievement for each student and the enhancement of a positive self-image. In addition to stress upon reading, math, and language arts, black history has been taught.

The program continues on Tuesday and Thursday afternoons and on Saturday mornings for a total of seven hours each week. It has been expanded to include an evening session on Tuesday and Thursday. Junior and senior high students are assisted with biology, math, English, and Spanish. Professional men and women of the church join with other volunteers in providing instruction. Beyond specific tutorial work these older students are provided counsel in vocational planning, writing resumés, making job applications, and in preparation for taking the Preliminary Scholastic Aptitude Test (P.S.A.T.) and the Scholastic Aptitude Test (S.A.T.), looking toward making application for college.

Scholarship Program

An annual college scholarship program is sponsored by the Business and Professional Women of Allen Temple. They have won the support of the church and larger community in this effort to recruit funds to assist college students from their church. The primary fund-raising effort is the popular fashion show, held annually in the Oakland Auditorium Theatre. This is the only fund-raising program the church allows; all other programs are funded through offerings. Apparently the effort receives enthusiastic support from business and professional people in

Oakland. An editorial in *The Oakland Tribune*, the city's leading newspaper, will help put this in focus.

> If you think it's hard to get excited about a church group fashion show, you haven't seen the one Oakland's Allen Temple Baptist Church puts on each year.
>
> Over 2000 persons attended this year's show. Sponsors raised $52,000.00 for college scholarships for church members.
>
> In the days when so many groups are asking for government handouts to solve their problems, the hard work that went into this show is an inspiration.
>
> Allen Temple Baptist Church members didn't ask the taxpayers to subsidize the needs of their children. They went out and did the work themselves—and did it well (April, 1979).

Similar amounts are raised year after year through donations and sponsorships of young men and women in the fashion show, which becomes a "fun" experience for all who participate or attend. The show, through a well-designed promotional book containing ads from sponsors and information about the program and church, provides an opportunity for the church to have an impact upon the community. One page is devoted to a very serious message from the pastor. In the 1981 book, the following sentiments are found:

> As a people you and I must struggle to raise ourselves above educational, economic, and moral bankruptcy. . . .
>
> At Allen Temple I have preached for ten years that we who are black must love and work with Hispanics, Asians, Native Indians, and poor white people because we share a common destiny. I have preached that God is concerned about every facet of life being saved from death, therefore Oakland needs a moral, economic, educational, and political resurrection from the grave of urban disintegration. I have tried to carry my ministry outside the walls of our church building into the streets of the city where ignorance

prevails, hate rules, and immorality prevails. I want our children saved mentally, morally, spiritually, economically, and politically. . . .

Let us teach our children that beauty is not in the clothes that models wear at this fashion show, but real beauty is in the spiritual quality of our morals, our mental state, our family life, and in our ability to build a better Oakland with persons of other races who are of good will.

The 1982 report of the Scholarship Committee reported that 54 scholarships were given, 42 to students in four year colleges and 12 to students in two-year colleges. The grants ranged from $100 to $750. Thirty-nine of these grants were to students continuing in college and 15 to high school graduates expecting to enter college. It is the work of the Scholarship Committee to receive and screen applications. They also assist the church in maintaining contact with the students and reviewing their progress throughout the year.

Not many churches of any size have as many young people going to college, and I know of none which provide this kind of assistance and encouragement.

Adult Education

Adults who have the desire for additional education are provided a year-round program of instruction. The course, taught by the pastor's wife, is basic reading, English, and math. It is attended by persons from three ethnic groups; some have not completed elementary school. They frequently have feelings of low self-esteem, and it is reported that the course aids them in developing a feeling of "somebodiness."

Spanish Study

The Hispanic population is the fastest growing in Oakland. A Spanish program has existed in Oakland since

1965. Through the family and youth ministries of the church, counseling, employment assistance, tutorial help, and a Bible class have been offered. Recently, Spanish language study has been offered at the church for English-speaking persons who would like to learn Spanish as a second language.

Released Time Education

An arrangement has been made with the Highland Elementary School for children in grades 4-6 to come to the church for special instruction in religious education one hour each week, October through May. The students who participate are volunteers and must have parental permission. The arrangements were made through an agreement between the Oakland School Board and Evangelical Released Time and is a part of a larger effort in the city. Approximately 60 students participate at Allen Temple; some are boys and girls who do not attend any church. A director and seven volunteers provide the administration and instruction. The course of study is based on the Bible, with the use of workbooks and emphasis is placed upon memory work. There are ten major assignments, and the pupils are encouraged to move through all. Examinations and report cards are used. City-wide competition is held twice a year, with top pupils receiving trophies. At Allen Temple they honor the pupils and staff with a banquet at the end of each year.

Special Classes

In addition to the educational emphases described above and all those which are a regular part of the educational program of the church, there are several weekday classes. The pastor teaches a Bible class at Thursday noon and another on Thursday night. There is a Bible class for children every Saturday afternoon. From time to time there are other classes of an educational and instructive nature related to other church programs, such as classes in drama, music, health care, and leadership training.

The church has an arrangement with Merritt College, a community college with an enrollment of about 10,000 students, to offer courses for college credit at the Allen Temple Church. From time to time these special courses are offered at night. They are available to their members and other community people who are age 18 or above and qualified for enrollment. The courses, fully approved and taught by certified persons, may be selected in the light of church and community needs. Courses in the leadership field have been offered in recent years, along with one entitled "The Bible as Literature." In California there are no tuition charges in community colleges. Enrollment in these courses has been between 35 to over 100.

Relating to Needs in Health Care

A rather recent new emphasis has emerged as a part of the program at Allen Temple. A Health Education Committee was established, chaired by a church member who is a Health Education Curriculum Specialist in the area of community health. She, along with another professional who is president of the Nurses Guild, led the committee to function primarily in the field of health education. The purpose of the effort is to develop healthy consciousness within the community regarding illness prevention and health maintenance. Their work has taken the form of maintaining a bulletin board containing posters, pamphlets, and information pertaining to health, providing bulletin inserts and announcements, and planning for occasional special programs and clinics at the church. Already increased awareness of better health care is being realized, and an opportunity for professionals in the health field to use their gifts in a Christian ministry is seen as valuable.

Community Involvement

Some special ways of working in the health field are realized as Allen Temple Church cooperates with other community efforts. They maintain, for example, an Allen Temple Blood Bank in conjunction with Alameda County Blood Bank. They recruit volunteers to work in patient services at the Highland Hospital. They assist in fund-raising efforts, as in the drive of the American Cancer Society. They provide space for dental and medical clinics. The church maintains a Cancer Screening Program run by a doctor and an administrator. A High Blood Pressure Testing Program is a part of the health service also. The Community Planning Organization relied upon churches, Allen Temple being one of the more prominent, for support, encouragement, and publicity in helping get the Health Center. It serves as a five-day each week health care facility in an area that does not have a nearby hospital and few practicing health professionals.

The church frequently gives recognition to its own members who are making contributions in the health field. Recently, for example, they designated a Sunday as "Dr. Israel Dunn, Jr., Day," honoring a member "for his leadership in providing mental, dental, and physical health services for low income persons in our community." In the health field, as in other areas, the church proves to be sensitive and caring.

Relating to Needs and Housing

Housing became an early concern of the current pastor of Allen Temple after his arrival in 1970. Records show that he appeared before the Oakland Redevelopment Agency in 1972 and complained that East Oakland had been "neglected and forgotten" by city officials. He said, "Our residents are in a state of despair, despondency, and dejection because the city seems to be uninterested in our problems." Among objects of his concern were inadequate housing for older residents and the inability of home-owners to get home repair loans. The newspaper account reports that the minister received a favorable hearing, and promise was made to look further at what might be done in East Oakland.

Pastor Smith was not to wait for others to act, however. He led the church to form a nonprofit housing corporation. This was the beginning of an effort that would finally see success in 1981.

Allen Temple Arms

Nine years is a long time to wait for the fulfillment of a dream. Soon after the nonprofit housing corporation was elected by the church they began to work with local, state, and federal agencies to try to secure funding and permission to build a housing facility for the elderly. After years of planning and frustration caused by delay, the pastor announced through a letter to church members on November 7, 1978, "I have good news to give you. The California Housing Finance Agency has approved our elderly housing site at East 14th Street and 81st Avenue for 75 dwelling units." He went on to express appreciation to officials and to members who had helped secure the approval, including the mayor of Oakland, senators, assemblymen, and congressmen. He added that plans would go forward to secure specifications for the building and contractors.

Part of the delay in approval, the pastor said in a news story in the October 18, 1979, issue of *The Oakland Tribune*, was related to the reluctance to approve a "ghetto location." But Pastor Smith added, "We live in the ghetto, there are elderly in the ghetto, and God is in the ghetto."

Funding in excess of $3 million was secured from the California Housing Finance Agency for the senior citizens' residence apartments, to be known as "Allen Temple Arms." On October 18, 1979, *The Oakland Tribune*, carried a picture of the mayor of Oakland, the pastor, and a deacon in the ground-breaking ceremonies. Contract had been made with a Sacramento construction company and the building got under way. Further delays and construction problems were reported, but in August, 1981, initial residents began moving into the housing complex. By October, 1981, all 75 units were occupied and have continued to be since that date. Dedication ceremonies were held in both August and September, and these were attended by hundreds of members of the Allen Temple Church. Prominent public officials from the national, state, and city levels were present.

Allen Temple Arms is under the control of a board of directors elected by the church. They have placed it under the management of the American Baptist Homes of the West. The resident manager, a member of the church, has been employed and is ably assisted by a maintenance engineer, a secretary, security patrolman, and several volunteers. Units rent from $48 to $242 per month, with rent being supplemented from donations. Residents must be age 62 or over and capable of independent living. Younger handicapped persons are allowed by permission. Eleven of the 75 units are equipped with wheelchair access. In addition to the apartments, the facility has central dining room and kitchen, lounge, hobby room, and library.

The church provides volunteer assistance through the services of a minister and several lay volunteers. A schedule of classes is maintained weekly, including Bible study, crafts, exercise, and other special interests. These classes are open to the public and are provided free of charge. A visitor to Allen Temple Arms is impressed with the beauty of the facility and with the efficiency of its operation. What a choice place for an elderly person to live, in close proximity to the church and in a spot of beauty in the midst of the "ghetto."

Community Improvements

Allen Temple Arms serves as an example of dedication and commitment of the church to the community. It also functions as an illustration of what care and effort can do in maintaining beautiful buildings and grounds. The church, through encouragement and assistance, lends emphasis to other personal and city efforts at maintaining clean streets and yards. Persons of the church, the pastor participating, occasionally take their brooms to the streets and sidewalks in a "sweep-up, cleanup" campaign. This encourages both the city and local residents to get involved.

Recently a garden club has been organized to beautify the church campus and the immediate neighborhood where the campus is located.

Assistance, both in a volunteer and low cost manner, has been given to some residents in efforts to make home repairs and improvements. Especially widows and elderly living alone receive this service, either through direct assistance or referral.

Relating to Needs in Employment and Economic Assistance

Any community faced with a high unemployment rate and a high percentage of persons in the lower income levels, such as may be found in East Oakland, deserves the special attention of a caring people. The Allen Temple Baptist Church proposes to serve as such a people. They take seriously God's concern for the poor. They join willingly in efforts to improve social justice for persons whose voices are not likely to be heard. They extend their own hands to those in financial need, and they accept them as brothers and sisters, treating them with respect and dignity.

Employment Assistance

The church makes a serious effort to assist those who become unemployed. This is done in several ways.

Regular efforts are made to learn of job opportunities and to post these on bulletin boards, insert them in the weekly bulletins, or even announce them in classes or from the pulpit. The names of unemployed persons, by permission, are sometimes shared with public groups so that the larger body may be alerted to the need. Referrals of persons seeking work are made to businesses, corporations, and service agencies. Letters of referrals, or telephone calls, are provided almost weekly in behalf of worthy persons.

In addition to this type of assistance, the Allen Temple Church makes special efforts in a highly organized way. There is a Job Fair Committee composed of resource persons from private industry, government personnel offices, and educational institutions. This group arranges and provides assistance especially to junior and senior high school students, college students, and recent graduates seeking employment. They provide instruction in career planning, job information, resumé writing, job application preparation, interview techniques, and other general counsel. Printed data from the Job Fair Committee is available almost weekly from the bulletin inserts and bulletin boards. A telephone number is available for persons to call.

Economic Assistance

Persons in need are not turned away from Allen Temple Church empty-handed. Through direct assistance of cash, food, clothing, or other forms of emergency relief a person may be helped. For others the help may come through counsel and referral. In 1981 the congregation gave $15,581 for their Food Box Offering and $17,699 to the Benevolent Offering. The food program is a cooperative effort between the Allen Temple Church and the Saint Louis Betrand Catholic Church. A freezer locker and other food storage are available at the Catholic Church, but each church has equal access to use the resources available. The Benevolent Committee at Allen Temple is responsible for screening the requests which come to the church for assistance. During a recent year, 210 persons were granted cash gifts, and over 700 persons were assisted with food. Financial assistance usually is for rent, medicine, other personal bills, and for transients. Investigation is made to affirm the need. Normally, assistance of a financial nature is limited to $200 per member request and to $100 for nonmember request.

Other assistance from the church comes through circles of the Women's Missionary Society, classes, and the Christian Social Concerns Committee. The committee sponsors an annual free Flea Market where persons may make selections of items. It also provides a minimarket each Tuesday where persons over age 55 can purchase food items at a reduced cost. In 1981, there were 1233 patrons of the minimarket. The Kaiser Corporation donated $2000 for support of the program. This was supplemented with many other contributions of cash and food.

Credit Union

In an effort to provide their people an alternative for both investment and borrowing, especially to free them from resorting to unwise loans through "loan sharks," the church has established a Credit Union. It was licensed in December, 1979, by the proper agency of the federal government. The Credit Union operates through a Board of Directors and maintains strict rules and audits as required by law. It is housed in one of the buildings owned by the church and observes limited weekly hours of operation to members. In early 1982 there were 525 depositors with the Credit Union. Rules show that to be eligible for a loan one must be a member of the Credit Union for at least six months. A loan application must be completed and approved by the Credit Committee. No board member or officer has the legal authority to promise or authorize a loan without the due process of application being followed. A ten-day waiting period is requested for credit checks and approval. Loans are made only for what are viewed as appropriate reasons and with assured security. Loans may be made in amounts up to $6,000 and for up to three years. Most loans, however, are for amounts of between $500 and $1500, and lesser duration.

Pastoral Influence

All of the programs described above have the encouragement of the pastor, who sees economic concerns of the people as vitally related to a healthy community. By his writing, preaching, and personal appeals and influence, he tries to give support to building a more stable economy. For example, on June 6, 1982, he wrote an "Open Letter" to all Allen Temple Church members in which he addressed "Our Plight Economically." Excerpts from that letter follow:

> During our recession Blacks and Hispanics are hurting. The Mormons are helping Mormons. The Catholic church is

helping the old Italian businesses in Oakland. The Jewish synagogue is saying "buy Jewish." *But our people are hurting.*
. . .

Our best young people are discouraged. Scholarship award winners finish school and are unemployed for months after graduation because other races and religions hire their own before they hire us. What can we do? What must we do? What will you do?

(1) Can we publicize minorities who are in business?
(2) Can we buy, sell, invest in minority enterprises?
(3) Could the women and men in Allen Temple, who are in business, provide summer jobs for our youth?
(4) How can we *build* trust and *diminish* jealousy?
(5) Will the business and professional people in our church meet and organize to help find solutions to our plight as powerless people?

The Board of Deacons has a committee on Economic Development. Please mail your ideas to Deacon Chairman Joseph Mondy or Vice-Chairman James Thomas.

The above letter is a method used by the pastor to try to sensitize the people and encourage those who can to act in the interest of improving the economic condition within their community. It further shows an effort on the part of the deacons to get involved.

Relating to Needs in Recreation

Most large urban churches have an active program of recreation, and Allen Temple is no exception here. Through various organizational structures and under different group sponsorships, an active and large program of athletics is carried on. Boys and girls, ages 10-12, make up the Little League Team. Boys and girls, ages 13-15, participate in the Babe Ruth Leagues. Under capable and dedicated lay leadership, these teams are viewed as being "character builders." The teams compete with teams of the city's recreation centers and boys clubs because there is no

church league in East Oakland. Allen Temple is viewed by
the Office of Parks and Recreation as being very prorecrea-
tion. One of the officials there declared that when they
wanted anything done in East Oakland, Allen Temple is
always used as a chief resource.

The annual athletic banquet is one of the big events for
the sports program. This is the time when awards are
given. Special guests include several of the prominent
professional athletes of the Oakland area, one of whom
belongs to the church and several others have attended
services there.

In addition to the league play for boys and girls, active
sports programs involve basketball, bowling, baseball,
softball, swim teams, and exercise groups. These programs involve persons of varying ages and many adults
take their participation very seriously.

One unusual feature of the athletic program at Oakland
is different from that found in many places. This church
program exists with very limited facilities owned by the
church. In Oakland, the city Office of Parks and Recreation
has access to public school grounds and gyms the year
round, when not being used for school programs. This
enables the Office of Parks and Recreation to schedule
events throughout the city. Allen Temple can have use of
facilities both indoor and outdoor as needed, simply by
scheduling in advance.

Besides athletic activities, Allen Temple gives support to
the East Oakland Youth Development Center, a program
the church helped establish by its support and encouragement. Many youth participate in activities at this center,
located not far from the church building.

The word *recreation,* in its broadest sense, includes many
activities beyond the sports field. Within the church, active
participation is experienced in Boy Scouts, Girl Scouts, Big
Brothers, drama groups, church camps, music ministry,

liturgical dance, and other programs. The mention of these activities by name is perhaps sufficient to acquaint the reader with the extensiveness of the programs available to the members of the church and community.

Relating to Needs Through Counseling

The counseling ministry of the church is under the guidance of the pastor. However, because of the size of the congregation and the increased need to assist persons facing problems, a team approach to counseling has been developed recently. Several professionals who work in the counseling and guidance areas have been recruited to aid the pastor in the overload he has experienced. Regular times for counseling have been established, but other sessions are available as needed.

Areas of need from which cases have arisen during the past year include school difficulties, drug abuse, family problems, marital preparation, teenage depression, suicide prevention, runaways, crime and incarceration, career development, and the need for spiritual support. Many of these cases can be handled by competent professionals from the mental health and social-work field. The church is fortunate to have such qualified persons within its membership to become a part of this counseling team.

In addition to these volunteers, there are other ordained ministers on the staff or designated as "ministers in training." These provide valuable assistance in crisis ministry and visitation. Further discussion of this will be reserved for a later chapter.

Relating to Needs in Citizenship Development

Far more than many congregations, the Allen Temple Baptist Church has a highly sensitive social consciousness. Perhaps this is due to the leadership of the present pastor for twelve years, and that of his predecessor, the Rev. C. C.

Bailey, who served from 1958-1969. For more than twenty years the present congregation has been exposed to preaching and religious education which has sought to develop social concern and commitment to Christian citizenship. The church has moved a long step toward becoming the kind of congregation these two pastors have urged them to be. The caring, servant role is one they wish to claim for themselves. And they are intent on trying to be the leaven that changes a community, the light that shines in darkness.

Hardly a sermon is preached without a note of evangelism *and* social concern. These two are not to be divided, but wedded. The cry of the prophet is heard calling for social justice. Education for citizenship, therefore, is present through the preaching of the Word. Seminars, special emphases, layman Sundays, recognitions, and all kinds of printed matter continuously hold the ideal of Christian citizenship before the people.

An illustration of this is found in the church bulletin for June 20, 1982. The pastor made an appeal for the members to be alert to opportunities to improve the economy of the immediate neighborhood. He concluded his remarks:

> Buy, patronize, clean up, paint up, fix up, sweep sidewalks and cut lawns in your community. Trust your people. Love your community. Build your community.
>
> Happy Father's Day!

Citizenship is seen as a way of life. The people are expected to involve themselves in the affairs of their city, state, nation, and world. They find ways to do so, extending from a local voter registration campaign to an offering for work in Liberia. They open their building to host a meeting attended by an overflow crowd they had encouraged to come. The meeting was held to "express concern for the mounting deterioration of living conditions" in East Oakland. The mayor of Oakland and several city councilmen were in attendance. The voice of the people was heard.

Allen Temple and other community parishes expressed their concern over the high infant mortality rate in East Oakland. They used their influence to work through the Community Planning Organization to secure the Health Center.

They were concerned over problems facing youth and joined in efforts to obtain the East Oakland Youth Development Center, and some of their members have always been on the board of directors of that agency. A group called Concerned Parents performs an advocacy role for children.

They were concerned over conditions in public education and joined in electing their own pastor to a position on the City School Board.

The church has been concerned with crime and the threat of persons and property and has established its own Walking Citizens Patrol, with two-way radios for quick communication.

The church has become known near and far for its involvement in society. The mayor of Oakland, the Honorable Lionel Wilson, said, "It is hard to think of any community action that hasn't been impacted by Allen Temple Church." He continued to describe that this impact came directly from the church or indirectly through the influence of individual members. He remarked that when they act individually, "They still identify themselves as from Allen Temple." Upon further inquiry, Mayor Wilson was able to mention five specific issues and relate the involvement of Allen Temple members to each one of them. With a smile, he added, "Fortunately, Allen Temple has been friendly to me." He also pointed out that the black community generally needed to get more sophisticated in their approach to social issues. The pastor of Allen Temple clearly agrees with this conclusion, and that accounts for many of his efforts to educate the membership of Allen Temple on matters related to citizenship.

There are churches whose theology will not let them involve themselves in the crucial social issues of the day. Their position is one of withdrawal, detachment, aloofness. There are others who conclude that there is nothing that they can do to impact the daily events around them, except as they evangelize. They do not know how, or else they refuse, to address the issues of social justice and civic righteousness. There are other churches who want to make an impact and they witness, pray, and serve, but not always effectively. I know of no church which so nearly implements its faith in the marketplace and seats of authority as does Allen Temple Baptist Church. Its influence in East Oakland and throughout the Bay Area is well known and deeply appreciated by many outside the church.

Conclusion

It should be recalled that the theory advanced in chapter 1 relating to how to measure the effectiveness of a ministry held to both a pragmatic test and a theological one. On the basis of these, the ministry at Allen Temple described in this chapter should be declared to be effective. Quantitatively, the church has grown, as will be described in the next chapter. Much of that growth must be accredited to both what Allen Temple *is* and what the church *does*. The image the church has in the city is one that has been established by the way the church's presence in the city is felt.

What about the measurement of theology? We claimed

in chapter 1 that the people of God on mission with Christ in the world should identify the purpose God has for them and then be true to that task. A church's effectiveness should then be judged by how faithful it has been to its theology and commitments. The theology to which Allen Temple commits itself, as described in chapter 2, was one that identified the church as being Christ's servant in the world for the purpose of the advancement of the kingdom of Jesus Christ. This chapter contains a description of many ministries that show the church trying to fulfill this purpose as it is understood by the church.

While perfection cannot and should not be claimed, faithfulness may be. Yet God's people must never be satisfied, and the Allen Temple pastor and people are not. They would like to be seen as pressing forward, yet seeking to attain. It is this sentiment that is found beautifully expressed in the closing words of the booklet, *The Local Church in God's Mission*. This booklet, coauthored by Pastor J. Alfred Smith and Mrs. Anna B. Vann, describes the efforts at Allen Temple. The concluding words from Mrs. Vann seem to express the attitude observed at Allen Temple. She writes:

> It is our endeavor to be alive in the world with feet on the ground going God's way. When we feed the hungry, clothe the naked, visit the rest homes by giving coffee hours, making lap robes for the wheel chair patients, contributing to the Chaplains' Fund at Fairmont Hospital, visiting juvenile hall, ministering to needs of the physical man as well as the spiritual man, we are striving to do His will.
>
> > "Master, when saw ye hungry, and
> > We fed Thee?" I can hear Him say,
> > "When you have done it to the least of
> > My little ones you have done it unto me."

We feel at Allen Temple we have a charge to keep for we know God's work is done through our hearts and hands. We strive to serve this present age, His calling to fulfill . . . all our powers engaged to do our Master's will.

6/Planning for Church Growth

Most denominations and congregations are interested in church growth. As long as masses of people remain outside the church, congregations ought to have a concern about evangelism and growth. This is related to the theology which motivates the membership of most churches. Christian people are committed to the work of preaching, teaching, and witnessing to the gospel in such manner as to spread the "good news." It is expected that if an effective witness occurs, church growth, at least to some extent, will be a natural result.

Church growth has become a "movement" in the United States, dating its origin to the year 1955. Peter Wagner divides it into three periods: The Incipient Years, 1955-1965; The Institutionalizing Years, 1965-1972; and The Years of Application, 1972-.[1] Much has been written on the subject, and congregational leadership would do well to study it. We will not treat it here in detail, but certain assumptions will be set forth that have been drawn from these recent studies.

One assumption is that church growth, in some fashion, should be possible for any congregation. Even if quantitative growth cannot be realized, spiritual growth should still be possible. To grow "in the knowledge of the Lord," to deepen ethical insights, to gain a more mature understanding of the "faith delivered unto us" are vital ways whereby any congregation may experience growth. The tendency is to think only in quantitative terms. The previous chapter documents growth for a congregation in terms of commitment and its concept of ministry. These are growth levels that should be pleasing.

A second assumption is that not all churches can be expected to grow numerically. Population mobility and decline, and other demographic factors, may be of a prohibitive nature. However, new growth through conversions should occur wherever there is a potential for it, and if demographic factors do not work to cancel the gains made, overall numerical growth should ultimately be realized. The extent of that growth must always be understood in light of potential, but potential can only become reality through the efforts of the congregation.

This leads to a third assumption. A church that desires to experience growth, either qualitatively or quantitatively, should act with intentionality. Growth is not apt to occur without intentional planning and effort.

Previous chapters have set forth some of the ways in which intentional planning may be done. A congregation needs to know itself, understand its community, and structure its witness and ministry so that it will best use its own resources and also address the needs of the people it wishes to reach. Planning takes place through enlisting and training people to be involved in ministry and witness. It consists of determining the kind of ministries to be pursued, and in establishing the organization and activities which will accomplish the mission.

Let us explore these areas through an analysis of the Allen Temple Church's planning for and realization of growth. That they have become a more mature group of Christians is obvious. Qualitative growth has been experienced and continues to be a major goal. The pastor and key leaders continue to stress the importance of spiritual growth, and this is one of the major emphases in leadership training. It has been reported also that quantitative growth at Allen Temple has been realized. In order to establish the extent of this growth some statistical data should prove helpful.

The church was established in 1919 and in 1920 recorded having 21 members. In 1981, the record showed a total of 2,872 members. How has this been achieved across the years? Table 9 shows this growth by decades.

Table 9
Membership Growth by Decades
Allen Temple Baptist Church

Years	Membership Change	Percentage of Growth
1920-30	From 21 to 37	76%
1930-40	From 37 to 81	119%
1940-50	From 81 to 273	237%
1950-60	From 273 to 409	49%
1960-70	From 409 to 1023	150%
1970-80	From 1023 to 2498	144%

Figure 2 helps portray graphically the rate of growth through these years. The greater acceleration of growth occurred between 1940 and 1950; growth continued at a lower rate during the 1950s when many churches in transitional urban areas experienced decline; and growth has maintained a strong rate during the past twenty years. The graph does not show it, but the church reported a loss of membership in 1978; this was due to a deletion of almost 500 names when the church rolls were corrected. By 1980 this loss had been overcome, and the roll is reported to be corrected annually since then, making the record more accurate. Since 1980 until the annual report in 1981, the church showed a gain of 374 members. This net gain is approximately 15 percent, which is better than the annual rate of most recent years.

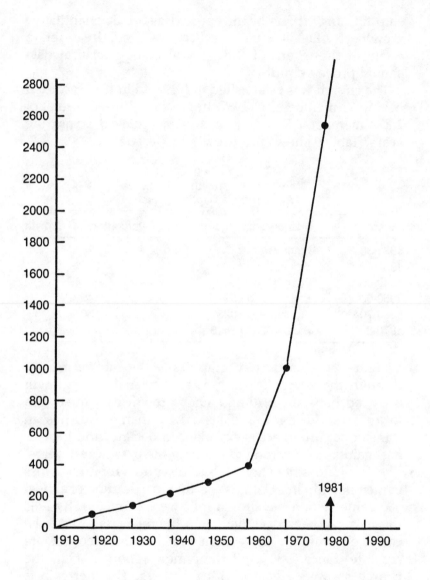

Figure 2
Numerical Growth of Allen Temple Baptist Church

How does one explain this kind of growth in an urban community where population decline and change are being experienced? If one will refer to the data in chapter 4, it will be seen that while the population in Oakland has declined, the nonwhite population in East Oakland has maintained itself in sufficient numbers to enable the Allen Temple Church to have potential for growth. Through their careful studies, planning and efforts, they have taken full advantage of these opportunities. Their steady growth is related to a combination of six factors which are discussed below.

Provision of Facilities

In 1977 the church made an extensive survey of the community and an analysis of their existing facilities in light of needs. They concluded that further facilities were needed, and they developed a "Program Report, 1977," in which they set forth needs for programs and facilities. In the 37-page booklet they outlined and described the needs for programs (ministries) to serve their own congregation and to provide outreach to the community. They established a valid case for the need of greatly expanded facilities. Since that date, some of this building program has been completed, but more is needed if all the projections from the 1977 study are to be realized.

As described earlier, a new sanctuary was entered in October, 1981. In addition, new provisions for all church offices, choir rooms, conference rooms, and several service rooms (such as for audio recording, printing) are a part of this building complex. The church already has experienced the benefits which come from these more adequate facilities. Before the new sanctuary was completed, the highest attendance for Sunday morning worship was between 1400-1600 persons when the combined attendance for two services was counted. Already in 1982 the combined Sunday morning congregations have numbered well in excess of 2000 on several occasions. Of course, and somewhat a surprise to them, they already have outgrown their new sanctuary for those Sundays of special emphases.

It is a fact that people will not attend a service Sunday after Sunday where they find themselves unable to find a seat. Adequate facilities are an essential for growth. The Allen Temple congregation must soon find a way to expand their educational facilities if they are to increase their Bible teaching programs on Sunday mornings. *Provide adequate space* if growth is to be realized in any program. This may be done through the expansion of facilities or through the duplication of services. Where a congregation already has two morning worship services, however, it becomes less probable that it will add a third.

Provision of Ministries That Meet Needs

As an earlier chapter pointed out, Allen Temple made a careful study of the community and then provided a network of ministries to service the needs they found. Some churches plan services and ministries only in the light of needs of persons already in regular attendance. They fail to ask the further questions: Who are people not now in attendance whom we should reach? How do we need to make alterations in our present programs so as to be more appealing to others? Allen Temple church has asked these questions, and as a consequence they schedule ministries and activities at suitable hours for some people they would like to reach. A noonday Bible study, after-school programs, and nighttime circle meetings are examples of these.

Perhaps far more significant than these modifications, however, are the community outreach ministries that are designed to provide a service to persons in need. The value of a ministry should not be determined by the number of people it may attract to attendance at a church service but rather at whether it meets a need. In 1977 Allen Temple listed 15 specific "community outreach" ministries which they would like to sponsor because these would address needs determined in their survey. Most of these ministries have been initiated and are now maintained as described in the previous chapter.

What has been the result? In primary fashion, most of these have been able to address the identified need and prove their value. But in a secondary fashion, these ministries have been related to the growth of the church. For example, hear the testimony of numerous members at Allen Temple who have joined in recent years:

> "The pastor and I became acquainted through politics, but then he enlisted me in the church."
> "I came to Allen Temple because I like the public image it had in the community."
> "It is my perception that it is the community extension that has built the membership."
> "Everywhere I went I heard about Allen Temple. I came to visit and kept coming back."
> "The knowledge and admiration of what the pastor and church were doing led me to come here. I belonged to another denomination."

These comments indicate clearly the by-product that comes from ministries performed in the name of Christ in a community. These ministries were not initiated to be evangelistic in the rather narrow, traditional sense of the word. They are, however, clearly evangelistic from the point of view of Allen Temple. It consists of *Being*, *Doing*, and *Saying* the word.

Evangelism needs to be understood in the broader

biblical and historical meaning, as suggested by Michael
Green. He stresses that evangelism contains three concepts: "The gospel is good news; it is proclamation; it is
witness."[2] A program of Christian ministry that demonstrates a congregation's willingness to give themselves in
service to a community is clearly evangelistic. When
troubled and needy people experience love and care in the
name of Christ, it should not be surprising to find them
attaching themselves to that caring fellowship. This must
surely be one valid interpretation of the growth that
continues to be realized at the Allen Temple Church.

The Use of Revivals and Special Services

In many congregations within Protestantism, revivalism
systematizes the process of evangelism and conversion.
For some, the annual revival is the primary means
whereby members are added to the church. While this is
not true at Allen Temple, the revival is a major asset. The
congregation enjoys good preaching, singing, and fellowship. Properly planned, the revival allows a congregation
to enjoy all three. At Allen Temple, at least two revivals a
year are a vital part of the program for church and
community. These revivals consist of nightly services, and
sometimes morning services. No particular month seems
reserved for the emphasis. For example, in recent years
they have been held either in January, March, April, June,
July, or August. Some capable minister, sometimes of
national reputation within his denomination, serves as
guest minister. It is not infrequent for the church to join
with another congregation in a joint effort, having services
at both locations.

Preparation for revival is made, making use of much
promotion, prayer, and efforts to enlist participation. Revival is seen as a means to provide spiritual renewal for the

congregation, as well as an opportunity to appeal to nonbelievers.

In addition to revivals the Allen Temple Church, perhaps in the tradition of black congregations, makes exceptionally fine use of special occasions and services. Easter, Christmas, and Mother's Day are three that receive considerable attention. Beyond these, however, are events that are highlighted and celebrated such as the annual Martin Luther King Celebration, Black History Month, Pastor's Appreciation Day, Children's Day, Anniversary, and other days as may be desired in a given year. These special emphases contribute to church growth because of the manner in which each is able to attract people from the community. When persons are encouraged to attend Allen Temple, for whatever reason, they are exposed to the beauty of the facilities, the warmth of the congregation, and the ability of the pastor and choirs. It is not unusual for one who comes for a casual visit to return again and eventually become a member. That is the actual testimony of many current members.

The Cultural Adaptation of Programs

It is a fact that many persons visit a church worship service or some other activity and never return a second time, because they find little there with which they can relate. When there is an absence of friendliness, an unfamiliar language, or a style of presentation that is offensive, a person may decide that church will not serve his or her need. We do not want to dilute the gospel with cultural entrapments, but neither do we wish to obscure the gospel through our inability to relate and communicate. Culture, therefore, cannot be ignored. One common way in which culture is viewed is to think of it as a style of social and artistic expression peculiar to a class of people.

Already we have declared that we do not want to be the kind of church that conveys to outsiders that they are not welcome if they are not like we are. One way of conveying this is to have the kind of service or program that by design ends up being exclusive. We do not exclude others deliberately, but they may exclude themselves because they do not and cannot feel at home. Our type of operation is so "peculiar" to our society or class that persons who are somewhat culturally different have difficulty ever believing they could belong.

This has always been a problem for the church. How can we make our services suitable for our own people and at the same time be sure that they are culturally relevant to those in our community we are trying to reach, especially when these people do possess cultural differences? This question has no answer apart from a particular situation. It is hoped that the friendliness of a congregation can be conveyed in spite of cultural differences. If genuine love and desire are there, perhaps the caring and warmth will show through. It is also hoped that the worship design, to be treated more extensively in a later chapter, can have enough variety within it that it can have an appeal to more than a limited group. By all means, it is hoped that a church will have the wisdom to provide suitable ministries which appeal to all the groups that exist in a community.

The Allen Temple Baptist Church will not appeal to everyone. However, the leadership has been wise enough to act upon the ideas suggested above in a way that has proved adequate to enable the church to have appeal to the people who reside in the community served by the church. Indeed, being more of a regional-type church, Allen Temple has considerable appeal for many persons who reside in more distant places. They have designed their services and programs, however, to address the needs of the people of East Oakland, taking into account the educational and cultural levels of the people.

Some churches in transitional communities function like small islands, isolated from the larger community. This does not appear to be true of Allen Temple. They continue to be able to appeal to people who live nearby, while still able to reach to the larger community. The appeal comes through the wide variety of ministries provided, and to the worship services which are theologically and culturally relevant to the growing congregation. The chapter dealing with worship shall expand upon this.

The Use of Evangelistic Invitations

In some evangelical religious groups, the public invitation to "come forward" and accept Christ as Savior is a common practice in congregational services. Historically, in many Baptist churches this has been associated with regular weekly worship services. It presupposes that there are those present who are not professing believers, or who need to make a public response. The invitation generally is expanded to include an appeal to individuals who may be Christians, but who are not affiliated with the church where the service is being held, to come forward and unite with the church "on the promise of a letter from another congregation."[3] The transfer of church membership becomes, therefore, a public action which is finalized by one congregation requesting and receiving a person's "letter" from another. Frequently, the invitation also appeals for "rededication" of one's commitment to Christ, and perhaps for a person who has been inactive elsewhere to become a member of a new congregation simply by a "statement of faith."

At Allen Temple, public invitations are a part of worship each Sunday and may also be a part of other special services, such as Bible studies and prayer services. The regular and repeated emphasis on persons responding in the various ways described above reflects a consistent stress upon evangelism. The congregation is conditioned to expect that unbelievers should be responding through conversion. They pray toward that end, and use their individual influence to appeal to their acquaintances to become Christians, or if already Christians to become members of Allen Temple.

In one of the training programs for members, the pastor has stressed the importance of evangelism—"personal, vocational, mass, and social action oriented." He tries to lead the members to put evangelism at the core of what they do in ministry and worship.

Through most of the years since 1970, more than 100 persons each year have been baptized into the membership of Allen Temple. In 1981, for example, there were 120, and in 1980, there were 110. Thus about 30 percent of all new members came through conversion and baptism.

Using Trained Leaders

No pastor or staff of trained ministers will be able to do all that is required in outreach ministry and witness in a metropolitan church. It should be viewed as the task of all Christians, the whole body of Christ. Training to engage in "life-style" evangelism, as well as in definite personal witnessing, is highly desirable. Not all Christians can be expected to participate to the same degree or with equal effectiveness. To some God gives the "gift of evangelist," but not to all. Peter Wagner says, "Research has shown that a church is in very good shape for growth if up to 10 percent of its members have discovered that they have the gift of evangelist and are using it in soul winning."[4]

At Allen Temple, much stress is placed upon training persons to function in evangelism. An active Evangelism Committee meets twice each month on Saturday afternoon. The group started in the 1960s and has had as its purpose to lead the church in an expansion of its evangelistic ministry. The 1981 annual report contained a list of 13 areas of service. Among these were participation in the church revival, evangelistic "street" ministries, visitation to homes of shut-ins and rest homes, letters and literature to those who visited the church services, the Tract Racks supplied with literature, prayer seminar and retreats, a 24-Hour Prayer Wheel, a course in Prison Ministry Training, and neighborhood Bible studies. During the early part of 1982, the committee sponsored a Spiritual Retreat, hosted the East Bay Evangelistic Conference, arranged for the use of a church van and intensified their efforts at street ministry and house-to-house walks.

The fact that lay people have been trained to function both in evangelism and ministry has no doubt contributed to church growth. Many people come to Allen Temple because some person from the church has encountered them through a direct appeal or ministry.

Conclusion

The elements discussed in the six sections of this chapter contribute to the growth of Allen Temple Church. They have been emphasized deliberately in the church. Through intent and planning, the pastor and people have moved forward together. In the 1977 survey they made specific plans and suggested some projections for future membership and attendance. In the light of community demographic analysis, and the assumption that the church would continue the growth being realized in the first half of the decade, it was projected that the church would have 5700 members by 1987, with one half that number in attendance on Sunday morning. The projections, however, were in error because they were based upon an inaccurate church roll. The following year several hundred names were dropped. Nevertheless, with membership now over 2800 and with attendance in 1982 exceeding 2000 on several Sundays, the goals may be more nearly reached than some would have thought possible. For 20 years, the church has averaged annual growth in excess of 10 percent. Last year the growth rate was 15 percent. With increased intentional effort, membership may increase even more rapidly. But if this is to occur, the ideas to be discussed in succeeding chapters will need to be taken quite seriously.

Notes

1. C. Peter Wagner, "Recent Developments in Church Growth Understandings," *Review and Expositor,* LXXVII, No. 4, 1980, 507-508.
2. Michael Green, *Evangelism in the Early Church* (Grand Rapids: Wm. B. Eerdmans, 1970), p. 48.
3. This particular expression is typical of Baptist congregations.
4. Wagner, p. 515.

7/Training and Using Committed Christians

In recent years many churches have made several wonderful discoveries. Kenneth Chafin specifies three:

1. "There are more people than the pastor. . . . The hope of the ministering church is the informed, inspired, committed layman."
2. "There are more days than Sunday."
3. "Sometimes a witness begins by meeting some need."[1]

These truths are vitally important. Gone are the days when the work of the church was done largely by the pastor on Sunday morning through proclamation. Every organized church needs lay leaders. Think of the roles to fill! We must recognize that God calls persons to function not only as apostles, prophets, teachers, healers, helpers, administrators, but as deacons, elders, musicians, members of the choir, those who work with children, and those who function in numerous and varied special ministries and do it every day and night of the week in season and out. To engage in witness and ministry is indeed every Christian's job.

For the average church which is committed to a comprehensive ministry, it is not easy to fill all the positions at the beginning of each new church year. To fill them with well-trained persons, or persons willing to be trained, is even

121

more difficult. It is an unending task, as persons die, move, become unable to continue, or simply resign for their own personal reasons. Recruitment of leadership is a yearlong task in the average church today.

The Matter of Motivation

When positions of leadership are filled with capable people, it is important to keep them committed to the role for a considerable period of time. This immediately causes one to consider the matter of initial and sustained motivation. How can persons who function as volunteers be encouraged to extend the duration of their service, and to serve with growing commitment and skill?

That question has absorbed the attention of pastors and researchers. Many Christians will begin their service in a local congregation out of a sense of obligation or "oughtness." They have responded to the call of duty which they have felt from urgent appeals, perhaps from the pulpit or from an approach made personally to them. The response to duty alone is seldom effective in providing sustained motivation. While it may keep a person involved in Christian service of a worthy sort, it may not keep one attached to a particular position of leadership. Job-hopping can be a constant problem which must be faced.

Some studies which I have made in recent years have helped me identify at least some of the ingredients of this problem. In a social survey of several hundred persons serving in volunteer capacity in the Louisville, Kentucky, area, I have discovered that duration of service is directly related to the sense of personal satisfaction volunteers receive from their service involvement. If they feel that what they are doing is important and that they are making a significant contribution, they are far more likely to stay in the position and serve with greater commitment. People need to feel good about themselves and what they are doing. There is nothing selfish about this. It is a natural need of human beings.

The question of motivation then is related to the question of what brings satisfaction to persons who serve in volunteer positions, and how can the satisfaction be sustained. The study which I made points toward some conclusions worthy of consideration by any pastor or administrator who needs to make use of volunteers.

Factors Contributing to a Sense of Satisfaction in Christian Service

Positive feelings about oneself and the work which he or she is doing influence the way in which a task is carried out and the willingness of a person to keep serving. At least four factors have been identified as contributing to creating and sustaining such positive feelings, and hence providing personal satisfaction.

Enlistment

The first factor is the manner of one's enlistment for service. From the outset one needs to feel that what he or she is called upon to do is a work of value that is worthy of the investment of the time and effort required. Sometimes people are recruited to engage in church work simply because the job exists and a person must be put in the position in order to fill the slate of officers or the committee membership. No sense of the value of work is mentioned. The way in which one may exercise his or her spiritual gift is not even considered. Indeed, on occasion the importance of the position may be depreciated, at least in terms of time and effort required, so as to get an affirmative answer from the one being approached. While this may "fill a position," it does not necessarily place the right person in the right position at the right time. Enlistment must be approached with great care and in a manner which presents a challenge, if the one responding is to feel positive about the job. Surely in church positions, consideration of one's gifts and where they can best be used for God should be objects of prayer and concern.[2]

Orientation and Training

Once enlisted, the matter of orientation and training for the place of service has proved to be vitally related to continued satisfaction. In the survey of volunteers in Louisville, the maximum job satisfaction reported was among persons who were perceived to have experienced excellent orientation and training. Those who perceived their orientation and training to have been only average or below were less satisfied in their work. Logic would seem to support this conclusion. If persons understand what they are to do and how they are to do it, it stands to reason that they will experience less frustration and disappointment. Most people want to feel that they are competent to do what is required. Orientation and training, when done correctly, can help enhance understanding and skills.

Environment

A third factor related to job satisfaction is the environment within which one performs the task. The general working conditions and the adequacy of the supervision are the factors here of most significance. People who are asked to serve need to be provided adequate facilities and equipment, if indeed their work is the type performed in a place and making use of equipment. One cannot expect to function well in the area of recreation, or music, or a Bible class, without some attention being given to facilities and equipment. In some other types of service, such as work in a youth center, a health clinic, or a craft shop, the matter of adequate facilities and equipment may be even more important.

The environment may also be dependent upon the kind of human support which may need to come through some form of supervision. Persons should not be left to work alone, with no one to show an interest in their work or to provide the necessary review and correctives. Sometimes, some churches are guilty of placing persons in important positions and never even inquiring about their progress or welfare until the time comes to reelect them, or to fill the position again. In every organization there should be provision for regular supervision. It allows for questions to be answered, needs assessed, skills developed, and support given.

Recognition

Finally, in the Louisville study it was found that job satisfaction was related to the extent to which the volunteer received appreciation and recognition for service rendered. Often even the most gifted person has difficulty assessing the value of his or her own effort. Some form of recognition helps immeasurably toward the feeling of contributing. There is something godly about the honest expression of appreciation to another human being. It may be given at intervals in informal ways, both by those who are recipients of service or from colleagues in ministry. Or it may be given in structured ways through letters of recognition, awards of merit, formal words in printed church bulletins, or at annual leadership banquets. In whatever way appreciation is expressed and recognition is given, these are among the factors that help "create" satisfaction and sustain motivation.

The Allen Temple Experience

A description of the extensive use of committed Christians in the church and community ministries at Allen Temple Baptist Church will serve to illustrate the four factors mentioned above. The adequacy or limitations of their efforts may be detected by the reader if they are not fully discussed here.

The Enlistment of Persons in Service

While not every member of Allen Temple Church is active in Christian service, this does continue to be a goal that permeates much of what the church does. There is an expressed theology that is enunciated by the pastor and many of the people that undergirds the concept that every member should be involved in Christ's work through the church. The pastor considers himself to be a type of "player coach." He wants to encourage "shared responsibility." When something may not go as desired, he says, "I will not let the people put the blame on me. They have to help me carry it." He has demonstrated that "there are more people than the pastor," and he has been able to convince a sizable number within the congregation that "the load must be shared."

This attitude of pastor and people is conveyed first of all to every new member through a required new member orientation class. My conversation with four new members who had belonged to Allen Temple between five months to one year impressed me with the way this sense of commitment begins to take hold. They said in common agreement, "You don't join to sit and observe. You join to participate." These four already had participated in new member orientation and a Leadership Training Seminar and were currently involved in the pastor's Bible study and teacher training. One had accepted a position in a Sunday School class, another on the Youth Committee, another in the Baptist Women's Circle, and one had become a deacon in training. Not all new members become this involved, but it is evident that the church's emphasis is there and a remarkable response is experienced.

The New Member Committee was organized in 1969 as an outgrowth of the Evangelism Committee. It's purpose is to provide adequate orientation to the life of the church and encourage each new member to become involved in a manner which will contribute to his or her Christian growth. The committee has worked through several formats but the current framework is for a program of instruction consisting of four class sessions offered during Sunday School to be repeated in cycles. Each new member is required to attend the four classes before being fully admitted into the church and given "the right hand of fellowship." The New Member Committee, consisting of 25 members, provides the instruction, using resource people as necessary. Such books as *The New Life in Christ* and *What Baptists Believe* have been used, in addition to prepared material entitled "Steps to New Member Orientation."[3]

Special emphasis is given to the church's organizations and the work of each. Particular attention is given to evangelism and stewardship.

In addition to the classes, new members receive other attention such as the New Member Mid-Year Fellowship and the annual Awards Night, honoring new members. Yearly anniversaries of membership have been recognized since 1973. An effort is also made to involve each new member in some service responsibility.

Besides the new member orientation and training, which serves as a type of continuous recruitment of potential leadership, the enlistment of Christians in service roles at Allen Temple seems to take several different forms.

Some are recruited annually, and at other intervals, through the work of a Nominating Committee and election by the church. Other persons are added to service roles through the self-expansion of committees which are encouraged to seek out persons who would like to join with them in their work. Indeed, some of the committees have become more like a "task force," a group of persons gathered around a mutual interest and seeking to serve in significant ways. While the committees function as necessary in the formulation of policy to recommend to the church, they are also working groups seeking to fulfill one aspect of the church's mission.

Another interesting way persons are put to work at Allen Temple is through a type of "self-appointment." Someone sees something that needs to be done and volunteers for the task. With permission when necessary, or by common understanding, the work is undertaken. It is in this manner that some of the current standing committees were brought into existence in an earlier day. The imagination and commitment of one person, or one small group, began a ministry which expanded the work of the church.

A final way of recruitment is through the constant efforts of the pastor, both from the pulpit and personally. He urges the people toward involvement. Frequently he suggests specific ways for an individual to become involved. Sometimes he designs new roles of service for the purpose of using the particular gifts of some member. The theology and philosophy of the pastor undergirds the enlistment efforts of all organizations and groups.

The Orientation and Training of Members

Already mentioned are the efforts with new members, but this is only a beginning. The main training efforts of the church are promoted through the work of the Leadership Development Committee. A 1978 statement of purpose for this committee lists four objectives:

1. Make decisions and take actions to train persons so they can respond to God in *faith* and *love* through ministry in the life of the church and in the world.

2. Develop mature Christians with a clear sense of mission.

3. Enlist persons and *properly* place them in the various church areas, so that the ministry program can reach its full potential.

4. Match needs with available resources.

In order to fulfill these objectives this committee, working closely with the pastor and minister of education, engages in certain activities annually and others as needed. These illustrations will show the value of this work.

A recent year found the committee reviewing and writing job descriptions for each of the chairpersons and cochairpersons for all boards and committees of the church. Copies were finalized and distributed.

In 1978, the church provided a three-day "All Church Officers Retreat" held at Clear Lake, California. The retreat objectives were five in number:

1. To strengthen the bonds of Christian fellowship and relationship between the leaders of Allen Temple Baptist Church.

2. To support the church's philosophy and program, as a unified body of Christian believers.

3. To examine, assess, and evaluate the ministries and organizational activities of Allen Temple Baptist Church.

4. To consider some recommendations and strategies for the 1979 church year.

5. To provide an opportunity for the church leadership to grow spiritually.

The program shows that they made a serious effort to accomplish each of the objectives.

The church could not provide a retreat like this one every year. Therefore, under the direction of the Leadership Development Committee two activities are held annually within the church's facilities. Potential Leaders Training Classes are held, and an All-Church Leadership Seminar is sponsored. The latter, in recent years, has been held over five or six Sunday evenings. The seminars consist of a joint meeting with presentations and pastor's lecture, followed by smaller group sessions for the study of a book, and completed with a joint session with worship. On the last evening there is a "graduation address" and presentation of certificates to all who have completed the study. Two books studied in recent years are *The Church in Bold Mission* edited by J. Alfred Smith and *Spiritual Leadership,* by J. Oswald Sanders.

Other training occurs, frequently using outside consultants, for committees or for persons devoted to a specialized ministry.

The role of the pastor in providing encouragement to leadership training cannot be stressed enough. The people are kept aware of his high expectations and constant challenge. On one occasion he wrote to the leaders:

> You who are elected leaders of the church influence the future, either with midget mentality or mighty motives. Your activity or passivity, your aggressive, forward, team-like, unified leadership of the members or your slow, retiring, fearful, lax, and relaxed attitudes can either give Allen Temple a bright or a bleak future. Hence, we cannot take our task lightly. Not only will the future judge us for our leadership or lack of it, but God, the Righteous Judge of Eternity, will scrutinize us with either the woe words of "Depart from me!" or the welcome words of "Servant, well done!"

The pastor has shared with the congregation his list of "qualities" which ought to be found in Allen Temple leaders, and "responsibilities" that ought to be fulfilled. Because those lists are basic to orientation and training, they are printed below.

Qualities of Leaders

1. A growing Christian
2. A loyal and informed church member
3. A dependable worker
4. A willing learner
5. An enthusiastic leader
6. One who loves people
7. A peacemaker
8. A student of the Bible
9. Dedicated to sacrificial service
10. A willingness to work with the pastor
11. Set an example as a percentage giver
12. Develop or groom an assistant to succeed you in office

Responsibilities of Leaders

1. *Communicate* by presiding, speaking, leading devotions and using public relations media.
2. *Administer:* Planning, organizing, evaluating.
3. *Instruct* by studying techniques of teaching.
4. *Demonstrate* through living, giving, witnessing, serving and cooperating in the spirit of Christ.
5. *Counsel* by listening, analyzing needs, and understanding and accepting persons.
6. *Keep abreast:* Use church library and attend Christian Education workshops.

Providing an Environment

The study referred to in the early part of this chapter addressed the need for good working conditions and adequate supervision. At Allen Temple provision is made for both, but in not as adequate a manner as they desire. Leaders of organizations, groups, and committees are highly respected and are invested with considerable freedom to function. In this regard a favorable environment is created. However, they do not always have either the facilities or the equipment that they might need or want. While approved programs are provided some funds from the budget, the amount does not always prove adequate, and frequently persons draw from their personal funds or attempt to raise money on their own. One does not hear complaints regarding this. Rather there seems to be an understanding of the limitations and a willingness to live within them or to search for an acceptable supplement.

From the standpoint of this observer, a more serious problem is in the realm of supervision. Some persons seem to be accountable only to the church and are left to function largely on their own. There is no professional staff which has the time to give attention to all details. The pastor cannot be expected to provide administrative guidance to the total program. He gives encouragement and support but does not have the hours which would be required to work closely with each of the varied groups. The minister of education, a capable and dedicated person, is a public school principal and a part-time church staff member, although he functions much as one in a full-time role. At best, there is no way he can be expected to give close attention to the work of more than fifty organizations, groups, and committees in the church.

The Allen Temple congregation is to be commended for the far-reaching and excellent program they maintain, largely with part-time professional staff and volunteers who give an enormous number of hours each week. One would not want to modify their sense of serious commitment and generous effort. One wonders, however, how much more might be accomplished with one or more capable professional staff persons working alongside their dedicated pastor.

Giving Recognition and Appreciation

One of the beautiful aspects of the ministry at Allen Temple is the way people care for each other. Very little criticism is heard, but affirmation is provided on every hand. The people appreciate their leaders and do not neglect to say so. Again, the pastor takes the lead in this. From the pulpit, in the bulletins, through written notes, and in face-to-face encounters he affirms persons and praises their efforts. He does this because of their dedicated service, but also on the basis of merit resulting from the high quality of their work or performance. Most persons thrive upon appreciation, and especially when that approval comes from the pastor. J. Alfred Smith does not seem to give affirmation as an "administrative device" to keep persons encouraged, but rather because it springs from deep within and is given with gladness.

Of course, there are formal and structured ways whereby recognition and appreciation are given. Mentioned above were annual awards banquets, special merit certificates, and special recognitions given in public congregational meetings. This latter expression may be related to a special promotional period inserted into a Sunday service. The recognition comes by way of introducing a leader who may then tell of the work he or she is doing.

Allen Temple is a church where fellowship is strong and mutual support is given. One guesses that the people may be following the example they have seen before them in their pastor. However, their behavior probably has become a fixed pattern by now—a pattern to be preserved, maintained, and through which God shall be praised!

Special Training Programs

At Allen Temple there are some unique programs not found at many other churches. One of these is training for persons who are potential deacons and is called "Deacons in Training." Also of importance is the role of the deaconesses and the way they recruit and train other women. A final program to be considered is under the sponsorship of the pastor and is called "Ministers in Training," a program for men and women already committed to ministry and functioning as ministers or for those who expect to become ministers.

There are 30 deacons at Allen Temple, ranging in age from 26 to 65. There is no limitation of time placed upon their service. New persons become deacons to fill a vacancy or to be a part of the expansion of the Deacon Board. In either event, they can be added only after having served as deacons in training. Worthy men are selected to become a part of deacons in training by a screening committee, in consultation with the pastor. They may observe a meeting of the deacons, meet in weekly classes to study the Bible and books on the role of the deacon, and fulfill such tasks as may be assigned them. These persons are observed for several months. When the need for the new deacons occur, the deacons and pastor select persons to be recommended to the church for election. Ordination may occur only if pastor, deacons, and church agree. The process has secured the service of several outstanding young men who have become excellent leaders even without becoming deacons.

Also serving in the church are 30 deaconesses. They have been nominated by a committee and elected by the church. Their term of service is three years, but they may be reelected indefinitely. Replacements occur due to vacancy for any reason or because of preference. New persons are assigned to work alongside an experienced person until adequate orientation and training have occurred.

Ministers in training at the time of this writing number eighteen persons. Within the group are those who are bivocational and those who are students. These persons vary in age, and both women and men are included. Because of their commitment they are highly respected by the congregation and given some unique opportunities to obtain experience by functioning in ministry roles.

These ministers work under the direct supervision of the pastor and receive instruction and assignments from him. In addition to numerous times when he includes them in training opportunities, as a general rule they meet with the pastor every week during the Sunday School hour. These sessions are occasions for instruction, sharing, and feedback. They are times when they give reports of work they have done and make inquiry regarding aspects of ministry they wish to have clarified. It appears that most of them view the pastor as their model and tutor, and they welcome the opportunity to learn from him.

Not only is this valuable training for these men and women, this organized effort adds greatly to the accomplishments of the church. In addition, they serve as a source of strength and support for the pastor and for each other.

One other training program of significance at Allen Temple is the Training Program for Bible Teachers. Persons interested in being used in this way have an opportunity to study in a special class under the guidance of one of the staff ministers. Each person also is assigned to a Bible class and works alongside the regular teacher both in a continuing learning role and in team teaching.

Conclusion

Persons interested in improving the quality of work with volunteers in church work should review the suggestions contained in this chapter and the example of Allen Temple Church. Of all the churches I know in more than twenty states where I have been, I have not found another where so many people give so generously of themselves and with such joy. Persons give evidence of their personal and professional growth and of their deepened sense of spirituality.

Notes

1. Kenneth Chafin, *Help! I'm a Layman* (Waco: Word Books, 1966), pp. 97-98.

2. Some good sources one might explore are these: John Hendrix and Lloyd Householder, eds. *The Equipping of Disciples* (Nashville: Broadman, 1977); John Zohn, *Discover Your Spiritual Gift* (Wheaton, IL: Tyndale, 1974); Wayne O. Harvey, "A Program to Help Members of the Archer Baptist Church Discern and Use Their Spiritual Gifts." Unpublished Doctor of Ministry Research Project, The Southern Baptist Theological Seminary, Louisville, Kentucky, 1979.

3. For another discussion of work with new members, see Lyle E. Schaller, *Assimilating New Members* (Nashville: Abingdon, 1978).

8/Celebrating Through Worship

Services of corporate worship traditionally have been the focal point of church activity in most congregations. Whatever other activities may be planned, a church is likely to be known and characterized by the nature of its worship service. Worship services, in whatever style they may be conducted, can serve as a unifying force within the membership, contributing greatly to the fellowship that is experienced. Worship is related to the purpose of the church, for through worship God is glorified, and participating persons are able to sense the power and presence of God in their lives.

Christian worship is indeed the communion of believers with God in Christ. It is the primary act whereby God is acknowledged. A worship service is an occasion that encourages attitudes of awe, reverence, praise, adoration, gratitude, and the recognition of the transcendence and dominion of God. It frequently contributes to attitudes of humility, penitence, and renewed commitment. Inspiration resulting from the communion with God, the fellowship with other worshipers, and the instruction which may be a vital part of the experience can lead to new motivation and decision.

Worship and theology are bound to each other. Emotion and intellect need to move in harmony. Praise of God should issue in obedience to his will. Indeed, the words over the door through which people pass as they exit from

137

one sanctuary expresses it well: "Be ye doers of the word; not hearers only" (see Jas. 1:22). Worship should create a desire to become a witness in the world.

Services of worship described in the New Testament were simple in form, and usually included singing, Scripture reading, prayer, and some oral proclamation, or what we today would call a sermon. Ritual in worship became very important in the early centuries. After the Reformation and the rise of Protestant denominations, there was some reaction to ritual and ceremony in worship. Churches today practice a wide variety of worship forms, from liturgical to very free and informal. The practice of an individual congregation may be determined largely by its own traditions, the preference of its members, and the choice of the minister or worship leaders.

Worship in the Black Church Tradition

Before turning to the examination of worship in the Allen Temple Baptist congregation, it will help to look briefly at the black church worship experience. Within black churches there also will be a variety of worship forms. In all of them, however, there is some uniqueness related to black preaching and black hymnody.

Black preaching is a dominant part of black worship which draws heavily from two streams of culture, West African and Euro-American.[1] Certain unique features emerge. Henry Mitchell claims that at least three characteristics can be detected.[2] (1) Preaching must be an *experience*, involving the totality of the preacher who organizes feeling tones around a text. (2) The concept of "Spirit possession," deeply embedded in African religion, is dominant with the black preacher who believes that the sermon, however prepared beforehand, is under the control of "the trialogue between the preacher, the congregation, and the very Spirit of God." (3) The black preacher will not allow "social distance between the shepherd and the sheep" but will make certain that he has identified with the people so that he communicates to them in words and tones that are not strange to their ears.

This type of preaching places great emphases upon subject and text, dramatic illustration, timing in delivery which frequently uses rhetorical devices and repetition to create interest and suspense, and the use of climax. Mitchell says, "the saintliest Black preacher knows his folk will go away with an empty feeling if he does not bring them to the level of the uninhibited celebration of the goodness of God."[3] True climax may indeed bring a type of ecstasy to the black congregation. The faithful preacher will want it to be not ecstasy for ecstasy's sake, but a time for empowerment to enable people to go with God into a hostile world and there survive.

While preaching is central in the black worship experience, it is undergirded and supplemented by music and song. Black people in America throughout the days of slavery expressed themselves in song. The spirituals continue to be seen as the expression of the innermost feelings of black people about God, their need of him, and their emotional involvement. After slavery, this type of music was expanded to include gospel songs and church hymns, especially some which suggest the theme of liberation. Always, however, the music used in black churches has emotion at the core. Without the emotion the music frequently fails, but with it the experience of the people reaches unbelievable heights.[4]

In worship services in black congregations, many standard hymns used in white churches may be used. However, most black congregations will select the major hymns from their own tradition, using spirituals or gospel songs written sometimes to the familiar tune of hymns. An example is a favorite, Dorsey's "Precious Lord," to the tune of "Must Jesus Bear the Cross Alone." In the singing of it, the congregation will not hear the words of the original tune but clearly will hear "Precious Lord." Black music is "created music," and the creation continues even into the act of the singing. It is designed to express feelings and to address human needs.

Preaching and music combine to provide the major ingredients for the black worship experience. While there may be many other unique features which can be observed and described, these two must be understood in examining the vitality of worship in the black congregation.

Worship Services at Allen Temple Baptist Church

Allen Temple Baptist Church expresses its purpose as being "the advancement of the kingdom of Jesus Christ" and attempts to accomplish that purpose through the pursuit of six functions. The first function listed said the church would "seek to attain this goal (purpose) through the public worship of God." The other five functions, while fulfilled in unique ways, are all related to worship, for worship at Allen Temple involves preaching, evangelism, missions, education, and an emphasis upon Christian ethical living.

The point being made here is that both by statement of purpose and in actual practice, Allen Temple Church has made worship central to everything the church does. Any casual study of this church shall discover that worship and preaching are the center around which all else revolves. This is not to minimize the other outstanding programs and ministries. It is to recognize that corporate weekly worship is the high hour for this congregation of the Lord.

Two major worship services are held each Sunday morning, one at 8:30 and the second at 11:15. They follow essentially the same order of worship, with slight variations. Normally the pastor preaches in each service, although at times he will preach only in one service with a guest minister or speaker being used in the other service.

In each service a deacon and one of the ministers in training are used to assist the pastor. Other deacons are assigned to assist in different ways, as with Bible reading, prayers, baptismal preparation, and sometimes with special announcements or presiding. Ministers in training are used to assist with communion and with baptism, thus providing the ministers experience and training in these ways. While the pastor may participate in worship leadership in any way he chooses, his primary responsibility is to lead the congregation in Scripture reading, preach the sermon, and extend the invitation to Christian discipleship. Most of the remaining leadership in the worship service is shared by those assigned for the day, who work alongside and under the guidance of the pastor.

A typical order of service on a given Sunday is listed below, although slight variations occur from time to time.

Organ Prelude
Minister: O magnify the Lord with me
Congregation: And let us exalt his name together.
Processional
Morning Hymn
Children Moments (a brief message to children who gather
    at the front of the sanctuary)
Prayer of Thanksgiving
Mission or Benevolent Offering
Music Selection by the Choir
Announcements and Acknowledgment of Visitors
Unison Offertory Scripture
Offertory Prayer
Tithes and Offerings
Unison Scripture Reading
Hymn of Preparation
The Ministry of the Word (Sermon by Pastor)
Invitation to Christian Discipleship
Closing Hymn
Recessional
Benediction

Examination of the order of service will show that audience participation is provided and expected. The response to the call to worship and the Scriptures are read in unison, with the congregation standing. The prayers are intended to express the needs and wishes of the congregation, who responds with the "amen" at the conclusion. The offerings, two each service, call for participation, with congregational members bringing their "tithes" to the altar. At least three hymns are sung, led by the choir but participated in by most members of the congregation. During the singing of some hymns, one can observe bodily movements on the part of some members through swaying or the movement of the head. Music is sung with feeling, and sometimes a stanza may be repeated because it is perceived that the power of the Holy Spirit is at work, and that the hymn has much meaning. The congregation continues participation in the preaching event, frequently expressing verbal response and occasional applause.

The service moves toward the high period of preaching. It is called the "ministry of the Word." The pastor, wearing a robe, mounts an elevated pulpit. He calls upon the people to rise, Bible in hand. In unison they read the Scripture. A "Hymn of Preparation," with appropriate introduction by the pastor and led by him and the choir, is sung by the congregation. At the completion of this hymn, there is a feeling of readiness, an air of expectation, which seems to prevail.

The sermon, apparently well prepared and carefully designed, moves to capture attention, develop interest, instruct and inform, show relationship to life situations, stir emotions, call for response, always weaving biblical truth, valid theology, and appropriate illustrations. The sermon builds to a climax and seems to carry the hearers to that high peak. And then it ends with an urgent invitation to respond to Christian discipleship. The call is to all—those who need to make an initial commitment and all others who need to renew their vows to faithfulness and service.

Pastor J. Alfred Smith is a powerful preacher. No guest preacher is apt to have the appeal to the Allen Temple Church congregation that Smith has. They respect him as a man of deep spirituality and unquestioned integrity. He has identified with them. He has walked the streets with them and shared their burdens. He does not hesitate to address any social issue of concern to his people, and like a faithful prophet he is always searching for a "word from God." He demonstrates concern and faith, and he preaches redemption, justice, mercy, and love. His message is current and earthy, both simple and profound. It is profound because he finds the theology and biblical truth which leads him to preach a valid gospel. It is simple in that he clothes it in a language that can be understood by all members of the congregation. It is a message that informs and educates. What is more, it inspires and sends people away with new hope and determination.

The delivery of Pastor Smith is a model. Blessed with a voice of rich bass quality, the pastor has mastered the art of dramatic appeal through voice modulation. He uses well his rate of speech, frequently resorting to pause and silence for effect or to repetition for emphasis. It can be said of him as was once said of another that his delivery is so masterful that "without being interested in the subject, one could not help being pleased with the discourse." When both content and delivery are of equal quality, a rare achievement has occurred.

It is not surprising that Sunday morning attendance continues to grow at the Allen Temple Church, and that overflow crowds are experienced at many services. This interest is to be traced to everything the church does to serve the people of the city. When persons come to visit, they are not disappointed because they perceive that here is a congregation that is authentic. Three aspects of worship, at least, contribute to this. The sense of fellowship among the people contributes to the worship experience, and strangers are made to feel welcome. The pastor's presence and preaching leads one to experience the presence of God in the place. The music, from congregational singing to the contribution of the choirs, soloists, and instrumentalists, creates an atmosphere where reverence and worship can be realized.

The music deserves further description. Allen Temple is blessed with several people who have musical skills which are being used effectively. There are those who can play the instruments, including piano, organ, and band instruments which are used to accompany the singing, but also to provide special effects. Quiet meditation, exaltation, or high excitement are created by the effect of music, and the instrumentalists can be thanked for this. Several choirs and singing groups take turns providing worship leadership through their music. Especially are these contributions realized when communion is served or holy days celebrated. Some voices are of professional quality, and these add greatly to the choirs. They also serve as soloists who never fail to move the congregation by their singing.

Congregational singing is a beautiful event. Some selections provide the mood created by a slow spiritual, while others are like the triumph of a mighty chorus. A considerable variety of music is selected over a period of a few weeks. To illustrate the point, the hymns listed below were used during recent Sundays.

"Lord, I Want to Be a Christian"
"I'm on the Battlefield"
"Sweet Hour of Prayer"
"Revive Us Again"
"Guide Me, O Thou Great Jehovah"

"Ye Must Be Born Again"
"The Lord Bless You and Keep You"
"Were You There?"
"At the Cross"
"I Am Thine, O Lord"
"Precious Lord"
"Lift Every Voice and Sing"

Hymnals are not used, but the words of each hymn are printed in each bulletin. The tune may be sung as originally written, or the hymn tune may be modified under the leadership of the choirs and instrumentalists. While the visitor may wonder at first how to join in singing, he or she soon feels comfortable with the arrangement. Congregational participation is such that it almost has the effect of becoming one mighty choir with a thousand voices. Small wonder that the inspiration abounds, and the presence of the Holy Spirit is felt.

Other Worship Occasions

Beyond the two worship services on Sunday morning, there are other activities wherein worship clearly occurs. As described elsewhere, Sunday evenings are devoted to services of a teaching or training type, or of a community service or ministry type. However, many more in recent months have taken on the form of worship services, but more informal than Sunday morning. Even so, some of the same qualities are to be found in any of the services as a result of the fellowship and music. The preaching is likely to be from one of the ministers in training, or a guest. If the pastor preaches, it seems that the sermon becomes more of special purpose type, perhaps devoted to teaching or maybe to evangelism. It is not possible, it seems, to build to the peak realized on Sunday morning. There is much value in the variety that is experienced.

At the midweek service, usually devoted to prayer and

Bible study, there is also the atmosphere of informal worship. Here too fellowship is experienced, closeness realized, and lives changed. Invitations to Christian discipleship are extended at these services, as they are on Sunday evening also.

Highlights of the year come in special services of revival which usually begin on Sunday and extend for several days. These are times of close fellowship, great singing of choirs and congregation, and usually preaching by a guest minister. Worship occurs, although a decidedly different format is used for the service.

One should not overlook those small-group opportunities for worship when a few people gather in a home, or maybe a room at the church facilities, and there pray together. Nearness to God and to persons may be realized here in ways that are never possible in the large gathering. Especially is this true on the Sundays when communion is celebrated. In the afternoon the deacons and deaconesses form teams and visit in the homes of shut-ins, serving the Lord's Supper to each. Not only is God glorified, persons are made to feel that they are a vital part of a congregation who loves them.

Conclusion

Because of the emphasis placed upon worship and preaching at the Allen Temple Church, it is understandable that the people respond so well and are highly satisfied. In the questionnaire administered to a sample of the membership, 100 percent reported being either "very satisfied" or "satisfied" with the worship services. Of all items to which persons responded, worship was seen as the most satisfying. Only a few had suggestions for improvement, but even they recorded themselves as satisfied. The suggestions were related to matters of personal preference. Eight persons felt there could be better time management in the worship services, perhaps taking only one offering instead of two and having less time given to announcements. The total length of the service did not seem to be a concern to too many people, but there was the recognition that the first service on Sunday needed to end in time for Sunday School to begin. This would allow one and one-half hours, and the feeling was that with more careful management the service could be held in that length of time. Some felt that the "clapping" should be eliminated from the worship service. This, they said, had been introduced by younger members in recent years. One senses a certain generation gap with divided preferences between applause and "amens."

Because of the congregation's high regard for worship, they have built a beautiful new sanctuary. It provides comfort and an atmosphere suggestive of reverence. No doubt the availability of this sanctuary has contributed to the increase in attendance at the two morning services. Further commitment of the congregation is seen in their resolve to retire their indebtedness within three years. They intend to honor God both with their lives and possessions.

It is very difficult for one not personally familiar with black culture to evaluate the black worship experience. It is evident that the nonblack members of Allen Temple are well pleased with their church and its worship services. It is also evident that white visitors to Allen Temple are impressed with the warmth of the service, the participation of the congregation, and the masterful preaching of the pastor. Some might come away believing that this indeed is a "black experience" and that such worship cannot be reproduced in the nonblack church. That may be true, but there is a larger issue.

Dynamic worship experiences need to be made available for Christians in every congregation. Allen Temple has achieved it. They may need to make alterations in light of the changing expectations of their growing congregation. For now, they appear to have achieved remarkable success at having worship services which are theologically valid and culturally relevant. This is the combination any pastor and congregation need to work to achieve. A service is not apt to have sustained appeal unless this happy balance can be realized.

The proclamation of the gospel needs to be made in the language of the people if they are to understand and heed. The particular cultural heritage of a people cannot be ignored without great detriment to the effectiveness of preaching. The educational, racial, age, economic, and social class characteristics of a people influence the way they listen, understand, participate, and respond. These factors should have a bearing in considerations given to the form of a service, the type of music chosen, and the content and delivery of a sermon.

This understanding has been applied by pastor and people at Allen Temple. To that degree we can all learn from them. We may not pattern our worship after their form and style, but we can apply the theory behind it to our own situations. To the degree that we succeed, we shall then be able better to lead our congregations in the worship of God, a worship that sends them forth to serve.

Notes

1. Henry Mitchell, "Black Preaching," *Review and Expositor*, LXX, No. 3, 1973, 334.

2. Ibid., p. 338. See also Henry Mitchell, *Black Preaching* (Philadelphia: Lippincott, 1970).

3. Ibid., p. 339.

4. Wendel Phillips Whalum, "Black Hymnody," *Review and Expositor*, LXX, No. 3, 1973, 353-355.

9/The Importance of Pastoral Leadership

While the effectiveness of pastoral leadership is difficult to measure, no one would doubt the importance of it. Indeed, it is safe to assume that behind every strong and effective church there has been a pastor who likely led with commitment and effectiveness. In this regard Brooks Faulkner said that poor pastoral leadership is like an ecological problem—difficult to see the damage until after it is done. Effective leadership is hardly recognized because the pastor may not be in the "parade," but has constructed the floats.[1]

It is obvious that an entire book could be written, indeed has been, on the title of this chapter. While space will not allow a full treatment here, any treatment of an effective urban church must give attention to pastoral leadership. At the outset, let us set forth some summary statements to establish a basis for an examination of pastoral leadership.

The Person in the Pastorate

The pastor is a person whose entire ministry is influenced considerably by the nature of his or her whole being and life-style. Ernest Mosley contends that wholeness is required for ministers to feel good about themselves and function and live with satisfaction.[2] He organized his book *Priorities in Ministry* around the desired affinity of the minister with God, spouse, children, church members, employers, and community. Clearly, a pastor whose life

149

causes him or her to experience each of these relationships will find that if they are well established and maintained with integrity, there will be a greater possibility of success both personally and professionally.

Most churches expect that their pastors will feel that they have been "called" by God, and that they will demonstrate through their lives a healthy and growing faith. The person in the pastorate, Henri Nouwen says, needs to believe that ordination does not create the person anew but serves as a recognition that the minister "has been able to be obedient to God, to hear His voice and understand his call, and that he can offer others the way to that same experience."[3] Everyone who comes in contact with the minister, Nouwen says, "realizes that he draws his power from a source they cannot easily locate but they know is strong and deep."

A great deal of the influence a minister is able to exercise, therefore, is not related to any particular function, but is derived from the personhood of the minister. It is related to what one is, as well as to what one does and says. Pastors do well to give care to their personal lives and life-styles. When they are married, attention needs to be given to their spouses and to their children when these are a part of a family. Most churches hope to find evidence of a happy married life and of a parental role being appropriately fulfilled. The pastors must recognize their humanity and take time for the natural human relationships which are a part of daily living.

Human needs, hurts, and weaknesses exist in pastors as they do in other persons. The despair, frustration, and loneliness that are a part of society are a part of the lives of ministers too. While they care for their own hurts and needs, they must be busy binding up the wounds of others. As Henri Nouwen reminds us, ministers are called upon to function as "wounded healers."[4]

The minister who is able to discover personal peace, and to balance the various expectations that characterize the ministerial life-style, will be much more likely to attain effectiveness in ministry. Part of the secret to this success may well reside in the inner directedness which comes from a relationship to God that has been nourished both by the sense of one's call and the sense of enthusiastic affirmative response. If there is a reluctance which negates the feeling of volunteerism, doubts and frustration may continue to prevent satisfaction.[5]

The Functions of the Pastor

Traditional roles for the pastor have been treated throughout the history of the Christian church. Inherited from the traditions of the religion of Israel were the roles of prophet and priest. Both continue to be a part of the present roles ascribed to ministers, although different terms might be used to describe them. Of course, many other functions have been added, as a study of any list of functions will immediately show. The particular functions of a pastor may well be determined by the nature of a particular pastoral situation, the ability and interest of a particular pastor, and the expectations of a particular congregation.

In order to have a frame of reference for our study, several lists of pastoral functions as treated by contemporary writers are examined. In Protestant circles, perhaps no single listing of pastoral functions has been used as extensively as that composed by Seward Hiltner in his book *Ferment in the Ministry*.[6] He points out that the contemporary pastor must lead in preaching, administering, teaching, shepherding, evangelizing, celebrating, reconciling, theologizing, and disciplining. Hiltner hopes that ministers will be able to find a sense of unity in the complexity of these roles.

Henri Nouwen treats the minister's role around five functions: teaching, preaching, pastoral care, organizing, and celebrating.[7] While the words and the meaning differ slightly from Hiltner, essentially they stress the same concepts. Under the role of celebrating, Nouwen speaks of the minister's acceptance of his own life and of the efforts to help others fully to accept their lives. The three components of the act of accepting are affirming, remembering, and expecting.[8] These concepts are cited here because they are to be treated later in our evaluation of the pastor's leadership role.

Pastors and churches are urged by Lyle Schaller to analyze the way members of a congregation think a pastor should place priorities upon the way time is devoted to specific functions.[9] Among the functions he treats are visiting, teaching, counseling, administration, evangelism, leadership in the congregation, leadership in the community, leader of worship and preaching, enabler, and denominational responsibilities.

While James Glasse would not necessarily deny the value of any of the functions to be found in the three lists recorded above, he selects certain ones which are to be viewed as absolutely essential. His selection contains the functions which may be considered the "rent payment" which entitles a pastor to go on serving within the parish.[10] These are: (1) preaching and worship; (2) teaching and pastoral care; and (3) organization and administration. Glasse insists that "paying the rent" should not be a full-time job, and that a minister should be able to find time for other functions. Ministry is more than maintenance, he said, and other roles may well prove to be as important as "rent payment." One new role for the parish pastor which is stressed by Glasse is that of "change agent," a role which may involve the minister in "conflict management."[11] He sees the importance of the pastor functioning as catalyst, both within the congregation and within the community.

From a careful review of the lists of functions recorded above, and from a wide variety of sources which space will not allow me to mention, it appears that Glasse's list of "essentials" will stand without question. Those who write on the subject place stress upon the functions of preaching and worship leadership, teaching, pastoral care, and administration. To these we would add the roles of change agent, or of leadership within congregation and community, evangelism, relationship with the larger religious communities, and the role of celebrating. The nature of a particular congregation and its statement of purpose and objectives are factors to consider as to how comprehensive the functions of a pastor should or may be.

Characteristics of Effective Pastoral Leadership in an Urban Congregation

This division of the topic being considered within this chapter may seem strange to any individual who thinks that the qualities which make an effective pastor in one location will serve to make that minister equally effective in another. This is a common mistake that some churches and pastors make. Because an individual has functioned well in one type of church or locality does not mean that he or she could do so in an urban setting which is considerably different. References to two brief case studies will help to illustrate the point.

Pastor X had been highly successful in a church in a median-size city in a Southern state. He had demonstrated his ability to lead in innovative ways, and his congregation had grown during the days of his ministry there. Partly because of his remarkable success, he was called to First Church in a larger city, located in a border state. Here he attempted to work in much the same manner that he had in his previous location. However, he found the people not as ready for innovative ideas, and he was unable to motivate them to respond. Growth which had come easily in the previous location did not occur here. Since he was accustomed to growth and now could not seem to achieve it, he became frustrated. His frustration began to show, and his relationships with the people began to sour. After a rather short pastorate he moved on to another location, in still another state. One pastorate had been considered to be remarkably effective, and the second was considered even by him to have been a failure.

Pastor Y served as pastor of a suburban church in a large city. The suburb was growing. Many military persons from a base nearby helped swell the numbers. The pastor, an aggressive, autocratic type, pointed the direction; the people followed. The church became proud of its good success and others heard of the performance. The pastor then accepted the call of a congregation in another city. The church served a pretransitional community which was beginning to experience considerable mobility of population. The congregation had a lot of very competent administrative-type leaders who had long been accustomed to studying issues and making decisions regarding policies and programs. The new pastor moved swiftly. Soon he had bypassed some of the established procedures and did not have the patience to allow committee structures to work. Interpersonal relationships began to be strained, and after one year the deacons let it be known that the pastor should look elsewhere for a congregation which might more nearly please him. He resigned in order to enter secular employment, and both he and the church had been greatly hurt.

Both cases serve to point to the fact that different churches respond differently to pastoral leadership styles. What works one place may not work well in another. It is even risky to suggest that one can discuss the characteristics of effective pastoral leadership even in a general way. Bearing in mind the variations for which we must allow between pastors and between churches, and at the risk of being more specific than is justified, let us establish some statements which may at least in a general way provide a basis for discussion of pastoral leadership. Nine characteristics will be identified.

1. In the urban pastorate, as in any other, a strong sense of response to God's call, a commitment to ministry, and a conviction that one is in the place where he or she ought to be will help provide the stability for faithful work. These attributes will contribute to the type of firmness that is required in the leadership. Others have stressed the need of a strong ego and the determination to see things through.[12] The pastor, they say, needs to be a type of "take charge" person, knowing his or her own mind and being sure of the leadership role. Sometimes I think others have excessively emphasized this, so as to imply that the urban pastor must be a strong, domineering type, even one who may insist on running the show. I would stop short of this emphasis because I think the best pastoral leadership is always democratic. Nevertheless, an aggressive leadership style based upon the convictions of God's leadership may provide the urban pastor the kind of confidence necessary in trying situations.

2. Led by God, the urban pastor needs to have a sincere love for people and the ability to care for and relate to all classes and types of persons. While some urban situations may provide ministry essentially to the same subcultural level of persons, the downtown church and many in other urban settings must be able to attract and serve persons from a variety of economic and social levels. Rich and poor, highly educated and those of limited education, multiethnic groups, those of varied vocations and interests, and persons of widely divergent life-styles all may be

found in many urban churches. The pastor must be able to love each, to provide ready acceptance and affirmation. Unless that awareness and sensitivity exists, the pastor will have difficulty leading a congregation to develop the kind of fellowship desired.

3. The urban pastor needs to be energetic and hard-working. This is no place for a shirker. If one is looking for an easy place to labor until retirement arrives, the urban church is not the place to look. The pastor may well need to be recognized as one of the hardest-working persons to be found in the parish.

4. Preaching is a function of the urban pastorate that carries heavy importance. The larger the church, the greater is the requirement for high quality in the pulpit. In smaller situations the pastor's personal caring for people, most of whom are known intimately, will more likely be sufficient to maintain healthy congregational life, even when preaching is considered below average. However, in the congregation where many people participate only on Sunday morning and seldom have personal contact with the pastor, it is in the act of preaching, and maybe a brief contact at the door, that they feel rapport is maintained. Of course, in the smaller congregation this may not be as acute, but the emphasis upon meaningful and effective preaching may still exist. Urban people frequently have learned to be critical and do not hesitate to evaluate preaching. They like to believe that their pastor is a "good preacher," and they are pleased to be able to tell others and to invite their friends to come and hear. The pastor who strives for excellence in preaching—in both content and delivery—will need to make this function a matter of high priority.

5. Worship leadership is another function which needs to come under pastoral direction. Some pastors pay little attention to this except for the preaching. This is a serious

mistake because urban people need the nurture of worship to sustain them through the stressful and difficult experiences that pervade urban life. Furthermore, the worship service is the first contact many persons who come as visitors have with a church. They need to experience a service of beauty, order, and reverence where meaningful worship occurs, and fellowship and identity with the church body is experienced.

6. The urban pastor needs to be a good administrator, giving careful guidance to the church staff if there is one, and certainly to the lay persons who volunteer their time. The church needs to be viewed as an integrated body of persons, all of whom are committed to ministry. It is the pastor's job to "manage that ministry,"[13] to see that Christians come from the "world" to worship and to be trained and empowered to return to the "world" to carry out their ministry under the lordship of Christ. The pastor may well function best as the "player-coach," to use Elton True-blood's expression,[14] or to be the "enabler." In the management of ministry the urban pastor needs to be one who is open to new ideas, is innovative and adaptable.

7. Teaching is an essential function for any pastor. It may have special meaning in the urban setting because of the varied interests and needs of persons who constitute some urban churches. Where the laity are to be used in a wider variety of ministries, more teaching, instruction, and training may be required. The pastor must either do it or get it done. Teaching of a biblical nature may be no greater in the urban church than anywhere else, but the application of that teaching to human situations will be far more demanding.

8. Leadership within the congregation will be realized through administration, teaching, and preaching, but this leadership will need to turn outward to the community, denomination, and world at large. Effective pastoral roles

are not usually realized in urban settings unless the pastor is willing to invest his energies and influence beyond the congregation. The pastor's voice needs to be heard in the city, in order to help shape the social conscience and stimulate social action in the interests of human welfare.

9. Pastoral care is always a function of the pastor and no less so in an urban setting. The pastor will need to function personally in this role as a shepherd and to supplement his or her own efforts through referral to professional persons. It becomes important for the urban pastor to learn how to use community resources which can greatly expand the services provided by the church.

Now the performance of the minister in each of these nine functions enables ministerial leadership to accomplish its purpose. The leader works for the people, but always with their consent. If they fail to respond appropriately, leadership may be said to be ineffective. Accepting the people for what they are, and in keeping with their expressed purpose, the leader seeks to motivate, inspire, equip, organize, and use the varied gifts of the people. When that leader is a Christian pastor, it is expected that the group will be pointed in a spiritual direction and under the power of the Holy Spirit move out to demonstrate that they are the people of God on mission for Christ in the world.

Pastoral Leadership
at the Allen Temple Baptist Church

The reader has already been introduced to Dr. J. Alfred Smith, pastor at the Allen Temple Church since 1970. Throughout the previous chapters the pastor's leadership has been described in ways related to the topic of the chapter under discussion. He has been seen as preacher, teacher, writer, counselor, evangelist, community leader, and administrator. Rather than to describe and evaluate further his performance in these various roles, it seems more appropriate to characterize him more generally as a person and as a pastor.

Pastor Smith, born in Kansas City in 1931, was educated in Kansas City schools and Western Baptist College. He received his B.D. degree in 1959 from the School of Religion, University of Missouri, and a Th.M. from there in 1966, majoring in church and community. In 1972 he received a Th.M. in church history from the American Baptist Seminary of the West and later earned the Doctor of Ministry degree from Golden Gate Baptist Theological Seminary in 1975.

He accredits two women, his mother and his wife, as having strong influence upon him and as continuing sources of encouragement and support. He uses frequent opportunities to give public recognition to them for the ways they have helped him. His mother is an active member of the church and is involved in community action. His wife, an adult education teacher in Oakland, also plays an active role in the church and community.

Dr. and Mrs. Smith have five children, one of whom is a minister on the staff at Allen Temple.

Ordained in 1951, Pastor Smith has experienced a varied career, including being principal of an elementary school, assistant to the president of Bishop College, Dallas, and two positions with the American Baptist Convention. For three years he was director of the Education Center in Northern California; for four years he was minister of community witness for the American Baptist Churches of the West; and for two years he served as field representative of the Ministers and Missionaries Benefit Board of the American Baptist Convention. From that position he became pastor at the Allen Temple Baptist Church.

With the full blessing and encouragement of his congregation, Smith not only has continued to advance his professional education but has served in some interesting capacities related to seminaries. He served as acting dean of the American Baptist Seminary of the West, in Berkeley, and continues there as a professor of Parish Ministry. Also he has been Adjunct Professor of Preaching and Worship at Golden Gate Baptist Theological Seminary.

In addition to his academic studies, the pastor has engaged in writing throughout the recent years of his ministry. His eighth manuscript was published in 1982 by the Progressive Baptist Publishing House. The book of sermons and addresses is entitled *For the Facing of This Hour.*

Smith is an active churchman within his denomination and beyond. Named Urban Minister of the Year by the American Baptist Convention, Smith has been in demand as a speaker and lecturer at conferences, conventions, and seminars both in this country and abroad. He has been vice-chairperson of the Board of Education and Publications of the Progressive National Baptist Convention and recently was elected second vice-president of the Progressive National Baptist Convention. He is a member of the Board of the Urban Training Cooperative of the Southern Baptist Convention.

It is, however, in his own city that Pastor Smith has given of himself so freely in service roles throughout the area. He is a current member of the Board of Directors of the Oakland Public Schools. He has been an active participant in more than forty groups in Oakland and the Bay Area, serving frequently as president or chairperson. These groups include ministerial associations, organized religious groups, educational groups, professional societies, and numerous secular groups committed to community improvement. These involvements have provided him a forum to express his own commitments to social justice, human welfare, and civic righteousness. It has not been uncommon that contacts made through these activities established friendships later proving to be valuable assets for Allen Temple Church. They also have provided a medium through which Smith and the church were able to speak to the larger community.

Pastor Smith has received more than 75 awards for local and national leadership. These awards bear glowing tribute to his extensive interests and the power of his influence. They have come as a result of his leadership in revitalizing the minority business community, reducing drug traffic, promoting youth employment, improving educational opportunity, extending civil rights, expanding health care, and generally enhancing communication across racial, social, and religious lines.

Among these awards are two which now are named after Pastor Smith and awarded annually for outstanding community service. These are the Associated Real Property Brokers, Incorporated award, and the New Oakland Urban Coalition of Business, Labor, and Minority Leaders award. In addition, the Easter Seal Society gave him the Humanitarian Award for 1981.

Mayor Lionel Wilson of Oakland in a private interview said of Pastor Smith, "I cannot think of any community leader who has contributed more to the greater Oakland community in community improvement programs." The mayor went on to describe how Smith was always out front in every worthwhile project, fighting for better education, law enforcement, more jobs, improved health programs. It was obvious that the Mayor was well aware of Smith's efforts. He described how he organized ministers around the city to promote a cause and how he got his own members to participate. "And when they get involved," the mayor said, "they let you know that they are from Allen Temple." Asked to explain how Smith and his members made their presence felt, the mayor called their approach very rational and understanding. He said, "When pressing the city to do more than it is doing, they do not do it in an offensive manner."

A member of the City Council of Oakland expressed similar appreciation for Pastor Smith's leadership role. He said the council had become sensitive to the churches and community groups and felt the influence of them upon some issues. Of Pastor Smith he said, "He is one of the most dynamic people I know. Some people you simply enjoy being around. Jim changes you!"

No doubt any characterization of J. Alfred Smith would have to focus primarily upon two roles: preaching and community leadership. Even many who are not members of the congregation will come to hear him preach. City leaders sometimes visit. They want to maintain contact with this man and his congregation. They do not forget what they hear, and they fall beneath the impact of the man and his message. Some have been known to come to visit and return to "join." Others, even of other denominations, return at frequent intervals. But aside from his obvious abilities to communicate in this format, the community leadership role is one which deserves more attention.

Smith is energetic and imaginative. He sees something that needs changing, and he sets out to change it. His connections, well established over twelve years, allow him to organize a coalition around an issue and assist mobilization of necessary resources in order to see important needs acted on. Sometimes an issue is addressed quickly and the ad hoc group disbands. Sometimes the concern is of longer duration and a continuing organization emerges. Smith has been known to initiate such groups, serve as the first chairperson, get the group underway, and then leave it in good hands and move on to something else. Frequently, members of his congregation have been recruited and continue in significant leadership roles after the pastor has withdrawn from that particular effort.

A professor of sociology at the University of California came into the church because of these shared interests in community service. He described how the church, under Pastor Smith's leadership, reaches out to meet people on the grounds of their interests and needs. The church, Professor Harry Edwards said, tries to help people discern and use their own skills within the larger community.

Dean Norma Tucker of Merritt College, herself not a Baptist, said of Pastor Smith, "He is my adopted pastor." She said she perceived that this was true for many professional people in the city. "He is the minister to them. We want his professional judgment and his affirmation."

"Smith is the outstanding religious presence in the Oakland area," said Robert Maynard, publisher of *The Oakland Tribune*. "He is not fragmented in ideology, but embraces his concerns in a way that fits together," Maynard added.

Smith is not a loner, as is true for many prominent urban pastors. Rather, he relates to the other pastors within his two denominations and also to those of other faiths. Indeed, it was among ministers of other denominations, especially Catholic ministers, that I found such high evaluation of Smith's work. They like his commitment and ability to work for community causes.

While the recognition has come to Pastor Smith from the larger community, he has not neglected his own congregation, and the members are very appreciative. This is shown through their growing responsiveness to the church, but also in their thoughtful evaluations of their pastor and church.

The chairman of the deacons, Mr. Joseph Mondy, strongly affirmed Pastor Smith and his leadership. He called attention to the growth of the church, and to the pastor's openness to people. Many of the newer members, he said, are persons of vision, ability, and dedication; and the pastor wisely uses them. Mondy described the pastor's leadership style and the way the two of them worked together to keep each other informed about concerns for the church.

The cochairperson of the deaconesses and president of Church Women United, Mrs. Ruth Young, has been a member of the church since 1953. She described how the church has changed and accredits the pastor with leading them in growth and in community outreach. The growth, she said, has led to changes in worship and some of their other services. "The church was more sophisticated when it was smaller," Mrs. Young said. She and others said the changes were related to the wider variety of people who are now in the church, and to the openness of the pastor to modify the form of the services to accommodate the needs and wishes of the people. This seems to bear out what the pastor himself said about the form and style of the worship service: "I believe church can be intellectually respectable and still have celebration and soul. We don't apologize for what we offer."

From the older to the younger, appreciation for the pastor was expressed. The sentiment of a sixth-grade girl expressed the thoughts of many when she said: "Pastor Smith is a prophet because he preaches God's Word. He goes around Oakland and helps the poor and elders. He builds apartments for the elders. He helps the community stop drugs and drinking. He's very friendly and considerate of people."

Formal recognition is given to Pastor Smith at each anniversary. In July, 1982, a celebration of his twelfth anniversary found the church giving Pastor and Mrs. Smith a special gift, along with a Friday through Sunday celebration. On another occasion they gave them a tour abroad. In 1975, when Pastor Smith received his Doctor of Ministry degree, the church honored him with a special Testimonial Dinner. The mayor of Oakland and two congressmen participated on the program along with several clergymen from the city.

Why all the acclaim for the pastor of a church like Allen Temple Baptist? It seems to come from a deeply grateful congregation and community because of the love and service the pastor has been giving all along. The nine characteristics of effective pastoral leadership set forth seem to be largely realized in the life of this man. They are framed in the life of one who in all he does, to use Henri Nouwen's concepts, tries to affirm persons, help them remember, and help them expect. He draws his power from the God who has called him, humbly accepts and uses his bountiful gifts, and has an insatiable desire to show others the way to the God he loves.

Not all of us who serve in urban places will be blessed in the same ways as the pastor described in this chapter. Not all of us will experience the recognition that has come to him—and it should not be sought for recognition's sake. We are obligated, however, to use the gifts which God has given us. We can strive in our way to demonstrate love for God and the city and for unreserved commitment to the high calling of God that has put us in the ministry.

NOTES

1. Brooks R. Faulkner, *Getting on Top of Your Work* (Nashville: Convention Press, 1973), p. 10.

2. Ernest E. Mosley, *Priorities in Ministry* (Nashville: Convention Press, 1978).

3. Henri J. M. Nouwen, *Creative Ministry* (Garden City, NY: Doubleday and Company, Inc., 1971), p. 106.

4. Henri J. M. Nouwen, *The Wounded Healer* (Garden City, NY: Doubleday and Company, Inc., 1972).

5. Faulkner, pp. 16-18.

6. Seward Hiltner, *Ferment in the Ministry* (Nashville: Abingdon Press, 1969).

7. Nouwen, *Creative Ministry*.

8. Ibid., p. 106.

9. Lyle E. Schaller, *The Pastor and the People* (Nashville: Abingdon Press, 1973), pp. 46-47.

10. James D. Glasse, *Putting It Together in the Parish* (Nashville: Abingdon Press, 1972), pp. 55-56.

11. Ibid., pp. 33-34. Other helpful material on this topic may be found in Larry L. McSwain and William C. Treadwell, Jr., *Conflict Ministry in the Church* (Nashville: Broadman Press, 1981); Paul D. Simmons, "The Minister as 'Change Agent,'" *Review and Expositor,* LXXVIII, No. 3, 1971, 359-370.

12. Ezra Earl Jones and Robert L. Wilson, *What's Ahead for Old First Church* (New York: Harper and Row Publishers, 1974), p. 69.

13. James D. Anderson and Ezra Earl Jones, *The Management of Ministry* (New York: Harper and Row Publishers, 1978).

14. Elton Trueblood, *The Incendiary Fellowship* (New York: Harper and Row, 1967), p. 43.

10/Dreaming New Dreams

However the word *progress* is defined it signifies change in the direction of a goal. An effective urban church wants to continue making progress. If this is to occur, that church will have to reevaluate and redefine its goals. It cannot stand still and expect to be carried upward, like some person standing on an escalator. For such a person, apart from some unexpected mechanical or power failure, the top will be reached without any personal effort. This will not happen for the church. A better analogy would be an individual climbing a series of stairs with occasional floors or landings that may signify the stairs turn a corner. The person will never reach the top without effort. Now and then he may stop to rest on a particular landing, but effort toward upward movement must return if progress toward the goal is to be realized.

The church that stands still will not be viewed as effective. The church is *not* to be a *static* organization, but a living organism. Movement, activity, and change are expected. The change may or may not produce numerical growth, as was noted in chapter 6, but change and growth in some areas of the church's life and ministry are expected. This calls for repeated efforts at reaffirming purpose, clarifying goals, and implementing new plans and actions. It may well require the church to dream some new dreams. The church that fails to do so runs the risk of losing its effectiveness.

New dreams for an institution can hardly occur without some serious attempt at evaluation. This book has referred to a process that leads to self-study and analysis. Remember the questions posed in chapter 1:

1. Who are we as a congregation? Who are we in terms of our human makeup?
2. Where are we as a congregation? Where are we in terms of historic time and geographic place?
3. What are we doing as a congregation and how well are we doing it?

When these questions have been addressed, researched, and answered adequately, the church is prepared to enter into dreaming, and even more—into structuring an intentional design for the future. The question is, in light of who we are, where we are, and what we are now doing:

4. What ought we to be doing as a congregation and how are we to do it?

The Basis for New Design

Evaluative efforts need to be pursued in whatever way is required to enable church decision makers to obtain the data needed. If that church's work has all been related to the church's purpose, as proposed in this discourse, the church needs to determine if that purpose continues to be valid. Have time and circumstances forced a modification? Probably not if the purpose is rooted and expressed in theological terms. In that event the purpose is reaffirmed, and the church called to fresh commitment.

One then considers if the fulfillment of the church's purpose has been sought along the lines of a "needs agenda." If what the church has been doing has been geared to the recognized needs of the congregation and the community, then the evaluation should attempt to determine if those needs still exist or if they have changed. Some needs may have been so specific as to have been met, and therefore they no longer exist. Indeed some churches seem intent on perpetuating programs long after the need for them has passed. Or perhaps needs still exist, but may have changed so much in their configuration as to require that the program or ministry addressing the need now should be greatly modified.

What I am saying is that evaluation of a needs-oriented ministry must determine if, in the light of changing situations, the ministry should now be continued without change, continued with modification, or be terminated. This type of periodic review is absolutely required if the work of the church is to remain relevant.

Types of Evaluation

Most congregations are apt to act simply on the basis of their own subjective feelings regarding a program or a ministry. Certainly congregational opinion is valid and should be sought. It should be solicited in a manner that will produce reliability.

Pastors, or other church leaders, have been known to design questionnaires, such as the ones reproduced in chapter 3 of this book. Such a design allows members to express their levels of satisfaction regarding the major programs of the church. Further study could then be made to determine the more specific reasons for dissatisfaction.

Others have used well-structured testing devices to determine the level of knowledge, understanding, or commitment on the part of members of the congregation related to the matters being studied. For example, Bible knowledge tests are available to determine how much learning is being accomplished in a Bible teaching program. Tests given before a series of study and then the same tests given after the study was completed are useful to determine the effectiveness of the teaching and the degree of learning. Evaluation of teaching methodologies

can be made in similar ways with one group being exposed
to a different method from the other.

In a questionnaire which was recently administered to a
sample of Allen Temple members, some open-end questions were asked. These were:

1. In my opinion, the *most important* "good thing" that
   has happened at Allen Temple within the past three
   years is:
2. The greatest disappointment related to the church
   within the past three years is:
3. If I had the power, the *one* thing I would change at
   Allen Temple is:
4. The most meaningful thing I have found at Allen
   Temple is:

In order of ranking the first three responses to question 1
were: (1) getting the new sanctuary; (2) building Allen
Temple Arms; (3) evangelism and growth. The top two
responses to question 2 were: (1) falling short of financial
goals; (2) less intimacy as we grow larger.

Question 3 had varied and wide responses, with no one
thing standing out. The top three responses to question 4
should prove very satisfying namely: (1) the strength and
support that comes from the fellowship; (2) pastoral and
spiritual leadership; (3) Bible study.

This type of data should help reveal where the people
are in their responsiveness and may point toward needs.

Of course, evaluation of the perception of needs is
especially useful in determining what ministries might be
most effective or the ones which would be best received. A
list of ministries can be prepared and persons asked to
check the ones of interest to them, or to rank them in the
order of their interests. Some churches have sent visitors
to conduct a door-to-door survey in selected blocks so as
to get a sampling of opinion from the public.

Interviews with knowledgeable persons in the community are useful in determining the problems and needs they perceive to be major at any given time. Much of the community study discussed in chapter 4 is the kind that should be made often enough to keep church leaders current in their assessments of ministry opportunities.

The emphasis here is not so much on an initial study that is foundational to beginning a ministry, service, or program. Rather our concern is with making whatever study is necessary in order to have some concept of how well a church has achieved what it sets out to do. This knowledge enables a church to turn the corner, or to start on up the steps. It must not tarry too long on any landing lest it become stagnant and fail to progress.

Beyond the self-study approach, a church may ask an outside consultant to make an evaluation and point out some alternatives. This has the value of getting an assessment that should prove to be more objective than any internal studies may be. Of course, the church may wish to consider carefully the consultative style of a consultant before establishing a contact. Some consultants simply try to determine what a church wants to do and affirm that decision. Others may collect data and then be very prescriptive as to what ought to be done. Still others may pursue a catalytic approach, assisting church leaders to examine their situation and reinterpret it, or at least look at all the possible alternatives.

Different situations call for different approaches. For myself, I think a fairly healthy church will profit most from the catalytic approach. Unless a consultant has had considerable time with a church, I doubt that he or she can provide a "prescription" with highly specific recommendations that will be "the final answer." I do think that a knowledgeable and experienced consultant can help church leaders look at several alternatives in a manner that may enable them to know how to take the next steps. The consultant also may be able to suggest possible alternatives which the leaders within the church would not discover for themselves.

New Dreams for Allen Temple Church

In 1977 the Allen Temple Baptist Church had a new dream, and they translated that dream into a plan of action. At that time the church made a careful evaluation of its programs, activities, resources and needs. As described through the previous pages, the church devised and implemented a plan for progress. The church has seen most of those plans and goals realized, and those that remain continue to be pursued.

The time to evaluate and dream is here again. Even as these words are being written, the pastor and church leaders are working on these plans. They are making use of an outside consultant who will serve as a type of external evaluator and catalyst. I do not know what will emerge, but in the light of past experiences it can be expected that this church will design appropriate steps toward further progress.

As a result of my own studies, partly based upon previous self-studies of the church but supplemented by interviews and participant observation and some data collection, there are some evaluative statements that seem valid. I will relate these to the six functions set forth in chapter 2 as functions which should be found in an effective church.

Worship

Of all the functions of the Allen Temple Church, none is fulfilled more beautifully than the function of worship. Chapter 8 has an exceedingly positive evaluation. However, as instructive and moving as the Sunday morning worship services are, close observation will reveal at least three types of persons present. These are the active participants—persons present and intently involved in worship. Then there are the responsive observers—persons who start out observing but get caught up in the experience, and for whom it may become a transforming worship event. The third group is composed of the apparent "onlookers"—persons who are present but take little or no active part in the service as far as one can tell. The goal of worship for the church is to lead all to experience spiritual growth, and the pastor and worship leaders work toward that end. With the diversity between the generations and the ethnic groups, it will continue to be difficult to design a service that is equally appropriate and pleasing to all. The service, as it now is, proves so effective that it would be unwise to experiment too much with it. Perhaps the conservation of time as related to announcements and offerings might be considered, a suggestion made by some of the members. Whatever is done, efforts should be made to maintain the balance that now exists between instruction, prayer, praise, and celebration. The pastor's preaching and the singing of choirs and congregation need to be emphasized as they are.

Evangelism

If the rate of growth experienced is to be a basis for judgment, evangelism is healthy at Allen Temple Church. The continued training of persons to work in evangelism in the city will need to be a strong emphasis of the church. Not only should there be a stress upon getting persons to engage in witnessing, but the quality or effectiveness of that witnessing needs to be evaluated. The church does not succeed in conserving and utilizing all new members. This may reflect the limited understanding and commitment of some who make professions and join the church. Or it may be related to inadequate orientation and assimilation of new members. Both of the concerns deserve further study and improvement. Indeed, both were mentioned by knowledgeable members as areas where more attention needed to be given.

Education

Of all the six functions under review, there is no doubt but that education is the one most in need of improvement. There are excellent persons serving on the Board of Christian Education who can take the lead in this area. With the growth of the church, there is an increasing need for an expanded core of well-trained people to function in leadership roles. While attention is given to leadership training, this continues to be a limitation. There are many good leaders but not enough, and the training offered is not sufficiently specialized to address all of the needs. This is not likely to change until the church develops the resources and commitment to add another well-qualified, full-time minister to the staff. There is no way that the present pastor can do all that is required in a church the size of Allen Temple.

One of the concerns of many of the thoughtful members is the need for better Bible teaching and more class time allotted to it. A significant step forward will be taken when Allen Temple develops a well-organized Sunday School, with well-trained Bible teachers, as well as securing adequate facilities and appropriate schedules to accommodate the classes. The pastor engages in teaching two or more Bible classes each week, and several other classes are part of the present Sunday School, but it still remains true that more than one half of the membership does not participate in structured Bible study. If this is to be expanded, it must be done by building a stronger Sunday School. Plans are now underway to retire the present church indebtedness and then move promptly to secure an educational building in accordance with the existing master plan for expansion.

Fellowship

Allen Temple is a caring congregation. Their services are open and warm, and a sincere welcome is extended to visitors and strangers. Benevolent concerns are stressed, and persons know that they can depend upon the church to share in time of need. They know how "to bear each others burdens." It seems evident that the New Testament concept of fellowship is realized here. Common support and encouragement are extended one to another in an attitude of understanding and love.

Evaluation of this function, however, will point to a concern for the future. For all the values that have come from the growth of the church, the size begins to be a problem. People can no longer know each other as they once did. It becomes far easier for a person to "get lost in the crowd." That is not the intention of the pastor or the members, and they try to maintain a spirit that will prevent it. However, unless a structure is provided that enables every person to be a part of a small group from which personal attention and support will be given, the danger of the loss of intimacy will continue to increase. Perhaps this need could be addressed through a well-organized and functioning Sunday School.

The need for further expansion of counseling efforts may be related also to fellowship. Unless troubled persons have adequate care their participation within their families and with the church family is limited. In spite of the enlistment of persons with specialized skills to assist with counseling, the pastor continues to be overloaded in this area of his ministry. It is a further place where an additional minister on the staff might provide some relief.

Missions

The church provides through the annual budget and special offerings for world missions. Much more attention is given to mission causes of a local nature than to more distant places. As opportunity allows, especially after debt retirement, the church would do well to consider a greater financial commitment through denominational missionary efforts. Missionary education could use greater emphasis than it seems to be getting.

Christian Social Ministry and Action

The two ways whereby Allen Temple Church may best be characterized are the congregational worship services and the community ministry efforts. Chapter 5 already has served as an affirmation of the church's efforts in ministry and social action. These efforts are extensive, comprehensive, and effective. Plans need to be made to continue with these commitments. Such efforts require continued research to detect new needs which should be addressed. They also require constant efforts to recruit and train leaders for involvement. The church is not apt to neglect this function in light of its past records of accomplishments and in light of the recognition which has come to the church from the city.

Other Areas of Concern

Beyond these six essential functions, mention needs to be made of other concerns expressed by members at Allen Temple Church. While conducting research there, I asked many persons identical questions, and the answers should provide insight for further consideration. One of my concerns was to try to assess how much the church was dependent upon the present pastor's leadership and what would happen to the church if for any reason he were no longer there. Anyone who has read the pages written in this book will recognize the considerable contribution of Pastor J. Alfred Smith, and may share my concern for the church's ability to sustain itself if he ceased to be pastor.

The answers of the people are encouraging. A thoughtful deacon was realistic in recognizing that if Pastor Smith should leave some members probably would leave also, because their interests and loyalties were largely to the pastor. However, he said, "Others would rally around" and renew their commitments and efforts. "Some people," said the deacon, "are not well anchored yet, and they may be here for various reasons." He felt, however, that the leadership of the church was intact.

Others essentially agreed. Some programs might be dropped after a while, they thought, because they were started and maintained largely because of the pastor's interest and support. But they added, "The Lord would provide another leader," and the programs would resume or new ones begin. Some older members were pleased to point out that with every change in pastors in the last thirty years the church had surged forward. They said this not to imply any desire for a change but to affirm their belief for the future. It should be noted that such an expectation, while hopeful, puts a heavy responsibility upon the next pastor. If one should come and the church not "surge forward," a certain "blame" might be laid at the pastor's door.

Pastor Smith expresses his own confidence that the people have been trained to carry on. He points out that he has tried to help the people to have a positive self-image and to assume responsibility. "I see myself as a player-coach," he said, "and I try to push my congregation into leadership roles in the church and community." He said the greatest satisfaction he experiences is in seeing persons accomplish a particular task he has prepared them to do. "I like to see someone come to bat and knock a home run."

Another question I addressed to these people whom I interviewed was to ask them to share with me their "dream for the future of Allen Temple." Many responded in ways related to one of the six functions treated above, and I will not duplicate their responses here. Some, however, added other "dreams" which are worth noting.

Some "dream" of being out of debt and having enlarged educational space. A campaign is underway to pay off the building debt so that this further need can be met. As in most churches, further growth in Christian stewardship is an apparent need.

Many, expressing some dissatisfaction with the public school, "dream" of the time they will be able to have a church day school. This does not appear to be a very likely prospect for the near future, if even a desirable one at all, when all other needs are considered. It will be better at this time to continue their strong support for the public school and try to improve the quality of this education.

Some of the members, expressing also a goal shared by the pastor, "dream" of a more spiritually mature congregation. The church, for many of the members, is the hub around which their lives reside. The pastor wants their participation in the social, political, educational, and other ministry activities; but above all he wants them to be firmly related to God through worship and prayer so that spirituality grows. True spirituality is difficult to measure, but one can predict that the desire for it in a church should be an unending quest.

Still other members are committed to leading the church into new community ministries beyond those already achieved. A recent evaluation made by a newly formed Task Force on Human Development points out some concerns the church will want to consider. The study group notes the lack of adequate coordination of the church's social service efforts and claims that there is not an efficient centralized management system. This results, they say, in competition among programs for internal and external funds, limited funding from external sources because of "sectarian" commitments, no unified development plan, and much duplication of effort. The Task Force proposes the establishment of a Human Development Corporation which will coordinate the existing programs and bring new ones into being.

It is too early to conjecture what will be the ultimate outcome of this study, but high praise is due to a thoughtful group of lay members who have focused upon some problems which need correcting. Congregations do need to avoid duplication and competition within their own efforts. Anytime a far-reaching network of services is established, such duplications are apt to occur. This is all the more reason for periodic evaluation and redesign. These kinds of studies are almost certain to lead a church to improve and extend the quality of its ministry.

Conclusion

As the Allen Temple Baptist Church evaluates where it is at this point in history and what new needs it should be addressing, it is discovering much for which it rejoices and gives thanks. But it is discovering also that rapid growth creates new needs, especially for organizational expansion and additional ministerial assistance.

Indeed, as a result of recent evaluations the church has made in connection with my own research there, it has been determined that much more emphasis must be placed upon coordination. Pastor Smith thoughtfully observes, "Everything we have built we can lose unless we get more coordination. We are at the crossroads."

253.22
B 471

70631

This is not an unusual feeling for a church that has experienced rapid growth and has found itself unable to assimilate and conserve its membership the way it would like. To bring about greater coordination of all church ministries it is anticipated that a new position will be defined, and that it will be filled by an experienced and qualified minister who can work to improve the administration of the church programs.

It is hoped that Allen Temple, like any good church, in its dreaming and planning will keep three desires in focus.

Continuity is one. Here is a church which has a past of which it can be proud and a foundation on which it can continue to build. From the past there is much that deserves to be preserved and extended. Every church needs a sense of continuity—something to love, cherish, protect, and thank God for. It serves as an anchor.

Change is another concept, and change is big at Allen Temple. For at least twenty years, they have been quick to seize new opportunities. They have demonstrated their ability to accommodate themselves and their church to changing circumstances. And they have been instruments for initiating social change in their city. As they plan now, I am sure that *change* will go on being a prominent word in their vocabulary. So should it be for every church!

The third focus should be a natural outcome of new dreaming and planning, namely *new directions*. For Allen Temple the map is not yet fully drawn, but the compass points the way. These people are committed to being the people of God on mission with Christ in the world. When they turn the next corner, they want to be sure that the road ahead takes them where Christ leads.

May new directions for all faithful churches do the same!